T0266218

PUTTING STAFF FIRST

A BLUEPRINT FOR REVITALISING OUR SCHOOLS

JOHN TOMSETT AND JONNY UTTLEY

First published 2020

by John Catt Educational Ltd,
15 Riduna Park, Station Road,
Melton, Woodbridge IP12 1QT

Tel: +44 (0) 1394 389850
Fax: +44 (0) 1394 386893
Email: enquiries@johncatt.com
Website: www.johncatt.com

© 2020 John Tomsett and Jonny Uttley

All rights reserved.

No part of this publication may be reproduced, stored in a retrieval system, transmitted in any form or by any means, electronic, mechanical, photocopying, recording, or otherwise, without the prior permission of the publishers.

Opinions expressed in this publication are those of the contributors and are not necessarily those of the publishers or the editors. We cannot accept responsibility for any errors or omissions.

ISBN: 978 1 912906 84 0

Set and designed by John Catt Educational Limited

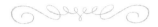

Dedicated to all our colleagues we have
worked with over the years.

And from Jonny to Skip, who inspires me still.

Achieving [a] better way [of doing things] takes recognition of, and moral outrage at, ineffective practices, confidence that there is a better way, and the courage and invention to find it and put it in place. **Roland S. Barth**

The quality of teaching is determined not just by the 'quality' of the teachers - although that is clearly critical - but also by the environment in which they work. Able teachers are not necessarily going to reach their potential in settings that do not provide appropriate support or sufficient challenge and reward. Policies aimed at attracting and retaining effective teachers need both to recruit competent people into the profession, and also to provide support and incentives for professional development and on-going performance at high levels. **OECD, 2005**

The first step towards making a person trustworthy is to trust them. **Seneca**

Reviews for *Putting Staff First*

Lawrence Stenhouse once described a curriculum as 'an attempt to communicate the essential principles and features of an educational proposal in such a form that it is open to critical scrutiny and capable of effective translation into practice.' I have often wondered what this would look like if we designed a curriculum for teacher learning with as much care as we strive to do for our students, and now I have my answer. Putting Staff First *presents the most complete and compelling vision that I have seen for a school that places teacher learning at the heart of its endeavours, rather than being bolted on as an afterthought. From selection and preservice education through to support for the most experienced teachers, John Tomsett and Jonny Uttley provide a clear template that any school leader can adapt for their own context, making it one of the very few books that I would recommend that every single school leader should read.*

Professor Dylan Wiliam

Putting Staff First *is an essential read for all school leaders. If we want to create the conditions for colleagues to do their best work for pupils, then staff have to come first. And this brilliant book shows us how - born of lived experience, it walks us through the structures, systems and culture which need to be in place to make this a reality: a hard-nosed look at creating the time for proper focus on teacher development; a proper, holistic way of approaching performance appraisal; the scaling up of disciplined inquiries; and serious attention to workload. Those schools that grow a reputation for staff development will find that recruitment improves, because high calibre teachers want to come and work in schools which put* staff first.

Mary Myatt
speaker and author of *Gallimaufry to Coherence*

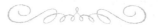

The combined practical wisdom of Tomsett & Uttley - rooted in their substantial intellect and experience - has provided a blueprint for schools and school leaders for the decade ahead. Full of supportive practical examples, Putting Staff First's *message is simple: develop the people who are developing our future generations. Great schools ensure their staff flourish; fit our own oxygen masks first, please.*

Stephen Tierney (@LeadingLearner)
Chair of the Headteachers' Roundtable
Blogger and author of *Liminal Leadership*

At last. A book for school leaders that inspires a collective endeavour where every member of a school team knows how much their contribution is valued. We hear of the vital importance of collegiate professional learning, of reducing unnecessary top-down workload and the energising approach of inquiry questions. Putting Staff First *shows what happens when we focus on building the learning capacity of our teachers so that our children can thrive.*

Professor Dame Alison Peacock
CEO The Chartered College of Teaching

Putting Staff First *is a powerful and beautifully written contribution to the debate about how we lead and improve schools. The most important job that any leader undertakes is to recruit, train and retain staff. Taking this three-part sequential journey as the structure for the book is no coincidence. John Tomsett and Jonny Uttley understand the relationship between embedding a culture of continuous professional learning and improving outcomes and the learning environment for children and adults. This book is a valuable contribution to the lexicon of thinking about how we lead and sustain great schools now, and for the years to come.*

Sir David Carter

Cutting through the widespread genericism of school leadership and tackling what really matters, Putting Staff First *is a crystallisation of all that is working within the profession. Both authors, exceptional leaders in their own right, combine forces to highlight the over-complication of many processes in our schools, and look to set them right. This book is more than a how-to for school leaders; it is a must-do for the education sector, if we are to sustain colleagues in a way that is both achievable and proudly humane.* Putting Staff First *is exciting because it will breed the calibre of leadership of the future that isn't just desirable, but essential to the success of our school system.*

Kat Howard
Author of *Stop Talking About Wellbeing*

It is an incontrovertible truth that schools matter and that they act at the frontline of our society in countless ways. For too long, however, teachers have been trusted but not treasured as professionals. Arguments over school types and structures have offered little beyond distraction. This book by Tomsett and Uttley cuts to the quick of practical ways forward. Putting Staff First *is part of a crucial movement to make supporting teachers central to our education system, treasuring our teachers by supporting them at every step of their career-long professional learning, and, by doing so, securing their personal well-being.*

Alex Quigley
National Content Manager at the EEF
and author of *Closing the Reading Gap*

Reading Putting Staff First, *written by two education leaders inspiring good practice in the north, is invigorating. For so long education embraced the certainty of the driven, ruthless leader who achieved success through a merciless drive for standards, regardless of the human cost. Here is a necessary rebuttal to those who lazily suggest a people-centred approach is anti-standards. This book will be a reassurance to any leader who has been told this modern approach lacks rigour. This is not really a testimonial, more a thank-you note for articulating what most of us felt but sometimes were nervous to express. Schools can be great places in which to work and be successful. This essential book shows you how.*

James Eldon
Principal, Manchester Academy

This is the book I have been waiting for! Tomsett and Uttley are true 'Talent Architects' putting great people management into practice and proving that this delivers for children. Putting Staff First *demonstrates convincingly that by prioritising their staff, school leaders will deliver the results they want for children. Drawing on credible research evidence, the book is packed with practical ideas, suggestions and models as well as great stories from the authors. The authors are highly credible and successful school leaders and this book is so timely in helping the sector tackle the recruitment and retention crisis. This blueprint is a must read for all school leaders.*

Mandy Coalter, LLB, FCIPD
Founder of Talent Architects
Former Director of People at United Learning

This clever book is more than the title suggests. It is a sustainable framework for school development and improvement that is rooted in people and relationships. And it is people and relationships that make schools thrive, especially for the most vulnerable students. Putting Staff First is a book for everyone and anyone in a leadership role in schools. You cannot dictate or bruise your way to sustained excellence. John Tomsett and Jonny Uttley demonstrate that the greatest way to positively influence our education system is through soft power, and enabling and encouraging others to be the best they can be.

Marc Rowland
Pupil Premium and Vulnerable Learners Adviser
Unity Schools Partnership

Putting Staff First is an invaluable book for leaders, teachers and other educators, at any stage of their career. Giving a reality check to the current climate we work in and using both research and their own wealth of experience within different settings, Tomsett and Uttley explore the notion of whether we are truly putting staff first. The book gives practical, step-by-step guidance and refreshing opportunities to reflect on how to make a difference to children, by ensuring staff are being the best that they can be, day in, day out, with the right support, encouragement and training at all stages of their development.

Cassie Young
Head of School, Brenzett CE Primary School

Contents

Acknowledgements

Jonny Uttley

I am enormously privileged to work every day with genuinely extraordinary people, and it is their drive, decency, humour and sense of common purpose that enable us to try to lead our schools the way we do. Particular thanks go to Lisa Pipes, our Director of HR, who is my sounding board and voice of reason and the person who makes our ideas about putting *staff first* into reality. Also, to Alison Fletcher, our Director of SCITT, who is the best developer of teams and staff I have ever met. I am hugely grateful to the rest of my talented senior trust team – Scott, John, Victoria and Jenny – who make it very easy to be brave and to try to do the right thing, as do our headteacher team, who lead their schools with real humility and decency. I am truly grateful for the support of Francesca, Charlene, Vicky, Sarah and Wendy, who make the place tick. And to Chris Abbott, who blazed the trail and gave me the chance to lead a trust. I am fortunate to work with a board of trustees whose values and ambition drive what we do and who buy into our belief that by putting *staff first* we create sustainable school improvement.

Finally, thank you to my strong, smart, funny daughter, Erin. She keeps me grounded, and her wisdom and wit inform a lot of my thinking about what a good school should look like.

John Tomsett

Huge thanks go to all those people I have worked with at Huntington School over the years, with especial acknowledgement of the contribution to this book made by: Penny Holland and Nigel Currie, who were directly responsible for developing the STARK materials and our performance development process; Jane Elsworth and the Research School team, whose evidence-informed work has been central to improving the quality of professional learning at our school; Garry Littlewood, whose leadership of curriculum development has been of inestimable worth; Matt Smith and Gail Naish, who implemented a new behaviour system with incredible effectiveness; Francine Russell and Paula Edgar, whose wisdom about all things Human Resources has been invaluable; Jo Olsen and the Huntington Governing Body, who share a humane approach to school leadership; and to my business studies boys and the 'Tomsett-Topset' mathematicians, for keeping me on my toes!

Beyond work, I am indebted to Tom Sherrington for his friendship and support, to my close mate Lloyd Brown for seeing our working lives through the same lens, and, of course, to Louise, Joe and Olly for refusing to give up on me.

Foreword

This book is a thing of beauty.

It is beautiful for those who care about children, for those who care about education and for those who care about the teaching upon which the education of the nation's children depends.

All of these statements may seem strange, as they don't say anything about staff – the substance of the book. However, as the authors say repeatedly with compulsion: without well-supported staff, none of the above is likely.

To someone who has spent her whole career in teacher development, this is such a refreshing message. The single most important in-school factor that can make a difference to children's learning is the quality of teaching. Without high quality teaching, children are so much less likely to make good progress in their learning.

The good news is – as *Putting Staff First* demonstrates so well – that so much can be done to support and improve teacher learning. All teachers have the potential to keep improving the quality of their practice. Both authors are enthusiastically and convincingly driven by the notion that good school leaders put *staff first* in the knowledge that this is ultimately the best way to serve the needs of the children. As I bounced my way through the pages of this excellent book, I found example after example of how to do this well.

It is also worth noting that this advice comes from the uniquely combined wisdom of a multi-academy trust CEO and a local authority headteacher. For me, this illustrates that school improvement is not about school structures but about people, support and motivation.

It is important also to hear the message loudly and clearly that putting *staff first* takes time, effort and unwavering commitment on all sides. Looking after your staff so they can do their job well is not a superficial activity and is so much more than pats on the head and coffee and cake.

This blueprint reflects (in my opinion) the heart of what we need to do to improve schools in England. It is written by two people I admire who have walked the walk and shown what is possible. They are leaders who are professionally generous and go beyond the tribalism which, it could be argued, has been encouraged in the recent past. They have a genuine desire to make the system better and offer some tried and tested practical examples of how to do this.

They do not pretend to have all the answers; the blueprint is ambitious and, in places, deliberately controversial. It is exactly what is needed to both stimulate an important debate and offer some constructive, practical ways to address the issues raised.

We all know that education is the foundation of civilised society and the single most important way to open doors and transform lives. Without teachers, we couldn't have brain surgeons, lawyers, and Nobel Prize winners. We wouldn't have well-adjusted people who create cohesive communities and make the world a better place. We need high quality teaching more than ever before. This means we need to put *staff first* and to do this with conviction and enthusiasm. Read this book and you cannot help but agree with me.

Prof Samantha Twiselton, OBE
Member of the DfE Teacher Recruitment and Retention Advisory Group,
Chair of the DfE Initial Teacher Training Core Content Framework Advisory Group

A note on the structure of *Putting Staff First*

One of the key features of *Putting Staff First* is that it largely ignores elements of the education system that are not within the gift of those who lead our schools. The future of school funding, for example, is for others to debate.

The closest we get to exploring something over which we do not have direct influence is the chapter on inspection, a chapter which says, essentially, that the best way to prepare for a visit from Ofsted (Office for Standards in Education, Children's Services and Skills) is for schools to do their job really well, every day, day in, day out.

Consequently, the scope of this book is limited to what school leaders can influence directly, and that, as you will see, is all about putting *staff first*.

At the Education Alliance, they have a simple school improvement strategy: 'The success of our schools going forward depends upon our ability to ensure we have a good teacher in every classroom, delivering an excellent curriculum, supported by highly efficient behaviour systems.' That strategy chimes perfectly with the findings of the OECD, which in 2007 was clear about the importance of the quality of teachers and teaching to any education system: 'A critical issue for any country that hopes to keep its education system internationally competitive is how to recruit, retain, develop and nurture a high quality teaching force' (Schwartz et al., 2007).

In organising this book, we have followed the OECD's mantra. We want our country's education system to be the very best, and we can only do that if we can recruit, train and retain a superb school workforce. To that end, we begin by looking in detail at how to **Recruit** the best people to work in schools. We then explore how best to **Train** our staff to make them even better, and then, in the latter section of the book, we look at how to **Retain** those colleagues we have recruited and trained.

At first sight, it appears that the *Recruit* section of the book is thinner than its two counterparts. That is explained simply: if schools *Train* colleagues well, those schools grow a reputation for staff development and they will find, as we have both found, that recruitment improves, because high calibre teachers want to come and work in schools that put *staff first*.

List of Acronyms

ASL   Assistant subject leader
ASCL   Association of School and College Leaders
CDG   Curriculum Development Group
CEO   Chief Executive Officer
CPD   Continuing professional development
DfE   Department for Education
EBacc   English Baccalaureate
ECF   Early Career Framework
EEF   Education Endowment Foundation
GROW   Goal, Reality, Options, Will
HMI   Her Majesty's Inspector
HR   Human resources
IQ   Inquiry Question
ITT   Initial Teacher Training
KPI   Key performance indicator
KS   Key stage
LA   Local authority
MAT   Multi-academy trust
MFL   Modern foreign languages
NASBTT   National Association of School-Based Teacher Trainers
NCTL   National College of Teaching and Leadership
NEU   National Education Union
NQT   Newly Qualified Teacher
OEDC   Organisation for Economic Co-operation and Development
Ofsted   Office for Standards in Education, Children's Services and Skills
PDR   Performance Development Reviewer
PDSA   Plan-Do-Study-Act

PGCE   Postgraduate Certificate in Education
PRP   Performance related pay
QLA   Question level analysis
QTS   Qualified Teacher Status
RCT   Randomised Controlled Trial
RQT   Recently Qualified Teacher
SAT   Standard Assessment Test
SCITT   School-Led Initial Teacher Training
SEND   Special educational needs and disability
SLT   School Leadership Team
STARK   Sociability-Thinking-Aspiration-Resilience-Knowledge
TALIS   Teaching and Learning International Survey (OECD)
TLF   Teaching and Learning Forums

Introduction

Putting *Staff First* - the rationale

The thinking behind this new book is best exemplified by an oft-used metaphor...

When cabin pressure falls inside an aeroplane and the oxygen masks drop down, parents are directed to fit their masks before they fit their children's. It is obvious why. Once hypoxia - a deficiency in the amount of oxygen reaching the brain - sets in, even the simplest tasks become impossible.

Symptoms of hypoxia vary from person to person, but include blurred or tunnel vision, hot and cold flashes, euphoria, numbness, tingling, apprehension, nausea, dizziness, headaches, fatigue and belligerence.

Without an oxygen mask, within a few minutes parents suffering from hypoxia will be incapable of fitting their children's masks, let alone their own. If parents fit their own oxygen masks first, it turns out to be better for their children, who have a competent, healthy adult to support them through what can be a challenging experience.

The parallel with being a teacher is striking. If we do not ensure, first and foremost, that our teachers are happy, healthy, well-qualified, highly motivated, hard-working, well-trained experts, they cannot be their best for their students. Consequently, a school that does not prioritise professional learning and managing staff workload - which, as a consequence, will help improve staff wellbeing - is disadvantaging its own students.

Whilst it is easy to say that schools would not exist if it were not for the students, the glib converse is that without truly great school staff, the students would not be taught well enough. What we need - as recruiting subject specialist teachers, school leaders and specialist support staff becomes increasingly difficult - is a revolution in how we treat the adults in schools.

'What is the most important school-related factor in pupil learning? The answer is teachers', say Schwartz et al. If they are correct, then we must put our staff before our students, because that is the only hope we have of securing what our students need most: top quality teachers (Schwartz et al., 2007).

The longer our schools are populated with hypoxic adults, the more we imperil all our futures. And whilst we are determined to put *staff first*, that does not mean working in a *blueprint school* is an easy ride; far from it. We expect teachers to work hard and to be the best possible version of themselves.

If high quality teaching is the only thing that really matters when it comes to improving students' outcomes, it follows, then, that we expect teachers in *blueprint schools* to accept the professional obligation to improve their practice; indeed, we consider this to be one of the most important aspects of being a teacher in a *blueprint school*.

I once had a chat with Professor Rob Coe. What he felt we are looking for in our schools is *leadership wisdom*, where policy and practice are based upon what years of working in schools and deliberate inquiry tell us about what has the best chance of improving students' outcomes.

The *leadership wisdom* you might find in this book is neither dogmatically based upon educational research evidence nor solely derived from our experience; it is a synthesis of both. What is common to *everything* we propose in our blueprint is that we unapologetically put *staff first*.

The *Cambridge Dictionary* defines a 'blueprint' as an 'early plan or design that explains how something might be achieved'. Ten years after the Academies Act disrupted the structures of the English school system irrevocably, we want to look ten years hence, to a revitalised school system where our nation's teachers are thriving and, consequently, our students are thriving too.

What follows is a 2030 blueprint to revitalise our schools that unashamedly puts *staff first*.

Putting *Staff First* – the LA headteacher

In 2014 I began writing my first book, called *This Much I Know About Love Over Fear ... Creating a culture for truly great teaching* (Tomsett, 2015). The title derived from a conversation I had with Leo Winkley, erstwhile headmaster of

St Peter's School in York, and Fiona Millar. I was explaining how we need to remove the real sense of fear from our school corridors, for both staff and students. Leo remarked that the opposite of fear was love, theologically; the rest, as they say, is history.

It was a book that swam against the cultural tide. It was published some five years after Michael Gove's Academies Act was brought into force, and a year after performance related pay (PRP) was made mandatory in schools. My attitude then was distinctly anti-academisation; our approach to PRP was that our teachers had to un-earn their right to a pay rise. More recently, those people running schools have largely accepted that changing school structures has little impact upon improving student performance (Robertson, 2018). Great teaching by great teachers is what makes the real difference to young people's lives.

I was surprised at my book's popularity. Its core messages resonated with teachers and school leaders alike. Now, in 2020, as we find it increasingly difficult to recruit high quality teachers, the mood is changing and, far from being an alternative view, much of what I wrote in 2015 is becoming mainstream thinking. That said, there is one important paragraph that I now believe needs amending:

One of the most obvious truisms about schools is that when it comes to educating students, teachers are your greatest resource. Any headteacher who explicitly puts the students first hasn't thought that decision through; the implication is that teachers are less important than students. The best thing for students is a happy, motivated staff; by putting the staff equal first with the students you are doing the best you can do for the students.

Five years on, I think putting *staff first* does not require qualification. I think we need to put *staff first*, period. 'Students first' is a misplaced sentiment, something recognised by Michael Fullan, who noted that 'children-first stances are misguided' (Fullan, 2008, p. 23). By putting *staff first*, you are on the way to providing for students the one thing that will help them make good progress in their learning: truly great teaching.

Furthermore, I do not think it is enough for staff to be 'happy' and 'motivated'. I think they need to be happy, healthy, well-qualified, highly motivated, hard-working, well-trained experts who, in return for the best working conditions we can provide, accept the professional obligation to improve their classroom practice.

As the decade has evolved, many friends in education whose work I admire greatly have become leaders of academies and multi-academy trusts, including a number from the Headteachers' Roundtable think tank. I chair York Schools and Academies Board, which is designation blind: all we obsess about is helping York's schools improve to the benefit of York's young people.

A school's status really does not matter. To use a common phrase, 'we are all in this together'. And every school's greatest challenge is to recruit great teachers. Even the major academy chains are finding it hard. When the flagship academy of one of the country's largest multi-academy trusts (MATs) was inspected in April 2019, it lost its 'Outstanding' label and was judged by the inspectorate to be 'Requiring Improvement'. In the trust's press release, it was made clear that 'the challenges that all schools are facing in recruiting teachers' was having a negative impact on the success of the academy.

We have a communal responsibility to help teaching in our schools improve, *right across the system*. Working on this book with friend and colleague Jonny Uttley – I am a traditional headteacher and Jonny is Chief Executive Officer (CEO) of the Education Alliance Trust – epitomises a third way of working. It is no cosy collaboration, but cooperation with mutually high aspirations to improve working conditions for all our colleagues, irrespective of the school structures within which we operate.

Working with Jonny confirmed for us how we are 'far more united and have far more in common than that which divides us'. As Chancellor Angela Merkel said in her 2019 address to the Harvard graduands, 'if we tear down the walls that restrict us, if we open the door and embrace new beginnings, then everything is possible'. Indeed, if we change the narrative and put *staff first*, we can revitalise our schools and secure a great education for our country's children.

John Tomsett, April 2020

Putting *Staff First* – the MAT CEO

In April 2019, The Snaith School – a single academy trust – became the fourth secondary school to join the trust I have the privilege of leading: the Education Alliance Trust. Snaith is a great school, deeply rooted in the community it serves, with a student body that is described by everyone who encounters it as 'lovely'. It was a significant moment for us, because this was a school judged 'Good' by Ofsted that was already an academy but was making a conscious and deliberate choice to join our trust.

When I went to speak to all the staff, I talked a bit about being a history teacher and what I love about working with young people every day. After the meeting, a member of the Snaith staff thanked me and said, 'If I'd realised you were a teacher, I wouldn't have worried about joining a trust and having a CEO.' It had never even crossed my mind that people might think I wasn't a teacher. I have gone from being seen as a member of one of the most trusted professions in the country to being viewed with all the suspicion with which an investment banker at the end of 2008 would have been viewed!

And this is a real problem in our system. For the last ten years, not only have we obsessed about structures to the detriment of what really makes schools better, but we have attached value judgements to people we don't know and schools we have never visited. So, if John Tomsett is an 'enemy of promise' to some at one end of the ideological spectrum, then I must be a cold-hearted business person to others at the opposite end. Indeed, on a bad day on edu-Twitter, I have seen people who I know have dedicated their careers to improving the lives of others called far worse.

If we move on from this binary nonsense about academies & MATs versus maintained schools, we start to see the reality of English education: there are great academies and great maintained schools; there are academies and maintained schools that are not so great; there are academies and maintained schools that draw teachers into the profession, develop them and retain them, and there are academies and maintained schools that drive teachers away.

A decade on from the dawn of Gove's reforms, the time has surely come to move on. What we offer here is a blueprint to do just that: a way of leading that can cut across the system and sustain and improve our schools for the next ten years in what will be a permanent mixed economy of structures.

I didn't make a conscious decision to lead an academy and then a MAT; it is just where I found myself. For what it's worth, my take on MATs is simply that good leadership in a MAT multiplies positive effects on more lives, while poor leadership in a MAT multiplies the negatives. But regardless of whether a school is maintained or an academy, the single most important school improvement strategy is putting the best teacher possible in front of students. It is the teacher who makes the difference, and that is why we need to put *staff first*.

The good news is we can train, develop and improve teachers. The bad news is we have too few and too many are leaving. Professor Becky Allen and Dr Sam Sims articulate perfectly both the good news and the bad in their book *The Teacher Gap* (Allen & Sims, 2019). Across our trust, we have made teacher development our number one priority. We are working hard to address all the barriers to teacher recruitment, retention and professional growth. We have looked honestly at teacher workload, recognising that it is not just the amount of work but the type of work that too many teachers are asked to do that disconnects them from their purpose. But there is much more to do still.

No amount of workload reduction will convince people to stay if they feel under constant surveillance and are held highly accountable while being denied the autonomy to change things. It is, perhaps, the worst kept secret in English education that teachers don't stick around in a toxic culture where anxiety has replaced trust.

John and I are two leaders in very different contexts, at opposite ends of the maintained school-MAT spectrum. What we share is a vision of how things can be across all types of schools. What we offer, after ten years of battles over structures, is a blueprint for the next ten years to revitalise our schools - one that puts *staff first*.

Jonny Uttley, April 2020

Part I - Recruit

The secret to my success is that we've gone to exceptional lengths to hire the best people in the world. **Steve Jobs**

1. Recruiting the best
John Tomsett

I was trying to recruit an assistant headteacher to take charge of the mathematics department. The person specification listed as essential 'a good Honours degree in mathematics, Class 2: Division 1, or preferably a First'. Of all the candidates who applied – well into double figures – just one met the criterion. Only two had mathematics degrees. In the age of big data and super-forecasters, if you have a good mathematics degree there are more attractive career options open to you than working in a secondary school earning £24,000 p.a. And as the number of great mathematicians who become teachers continues to dwindle, we will surely see a decline in the quality of mathematics teaching in our schools, which will mean fewer good mathematicians attaining degrees in the subject, and so the downward spiral gathers momentum...

There is a limit to what individual school leaders can do to recruit great teachers to their schools, and to attract great people to the teaching profession more generally. One seemingly obvious way to recruit the best to your school is to pay recruits more than the accepted national rates for individual posts. But this recruitment strategy is not an option for the vast majority of school leaders. We are in the business of educating the masses at scale. Class sizes are maximised. Teaching loads are full. Every penny is counted. And over the next ten years, it is unlikely that school funding will grow in real terms.

It follows that if we are going to improve recruitment to our individual schools and to the profession as a whole, we have to put *staff first*. And that means combining all the elements of this book into a coherent whole. This means treating teachers with respect by training them to be professionals who are intelligently deliberate about improving their practice, who understand the learning process at a profound level, who are experts in their disciplinary field and accept the professional obligation to improve, who are allowed to thrive because unnecessary activities are eliminated from their working lives, whose workload is made manageable because it is reduced to its essential core, who work in schools where the leadership team's main purpose is to remove any barriers preventing them from teaching as well as they possibly can, and whose place of work is one where the leadership team treat every single member of staff with humanity.

At the core of that coherent whole is the development of the individual teacher. We have found that our evidence-informed approach to developing staff, with 70+ hours of ring-fenced professional development time, has proved to be attractive to candidates responding to adverts for vacancies. It is an indication to potential colleagues that we prioritise teacher learning. Indeed, if we can consistently put the professional development needs of *staff first*, then we can revitalise our schools and will have a chance of improving recruitment and retention in our profession.

Thinking about recruitment in more detail, there are several elements of the teacher recruitment process that can be managed in a way which helps identify the best possible person for the post and puts the immediate needs of the candidates first.

Before we go any further, it is, perhaps, worth being very open with candidates about the main features of the culture you are attempting to create at your school, so that you have a 'cultural fit' against which you can judge the candidates, and a description of the institutional culture they can reflect upon before deciding whether they would want to work at your school. Writing this, I was reminded of a piece by the wise and wonderful Doug Lemov and his thoughts around recruitment and cultural fit (Lemov, 2015a). For all of us involved in both recruiting and seeking a career move, it is an important read. It prompted me to construct the document below, which details for our prospective candidates the core of what we believe in at Huntington. I hand it to them to read at the beginning of the interview day:

HUNTINGTON SCHOOL

Huntington School's Cultural Fit

Working in a school where you are not aligned with the culture is a miserable experience. So ... we *both* need to have alignment if you come to work here!

- We believe that staff come first.
- We believe that we all have a professional obligation to improve as teachers.
- We believe that every child deserves a Champion.
- We believe in a culture of the possible, where we can all make progress beyond what anyone, including ourselves, could have imagined.
- We believe that truly great teaching is that which improves students' progress.
- We believe an evidence-informed approach to teaching and learning helps us identify what works best in the classroom.
- We believe that hard work is the key to success for staff and students.
- We believe that you cannot just wish teachers and students to be better - you have to create the conditions for them to grow.
- We believe basic literacy and numeracy are essential to students making good progress.
- We welcome diverse ideas to solve problems.
- We believe that feedback should be timely and respond to the needs of the individual student so that they can actively engage with the feedback.
- We value generosity of spirit.
- We acknowledge that we all make mistakes.
- We live by the values of Respect, Honesty and Kindness.

Teacher development is most effective when it is embedded in a school culture where teachers and leaders speak a common technical language, are determined (and humble) about getting better, and feel a bit of urgency. In that environment, a great workshop, feedback from a colleague, or a bit of lesson study all have a good chance of driving improvement. Without it, our efforts tend to founder. In other words, the culture in which teacher development occurs is the biggest driver of improvement.   **Doug Lemov**

As it says, if the cultural fit is not right, it will be a miserable experience for both employer and employee. During the course of the day, if the candidate feels uncomfortable with what we are and what we believe in, then they should say so and we can part friends. As Lemov writes, '[n]o one wants to spend their career at odds with the organization they work for, trying to hide from the training it offers, or watching the philosophy change every year while thinking, *this too shall pass.*' (Lemov, 2015a).

It is important that the successful candidate feels able to operate within the culture of your school. Appointing someone who is unaware of your cultural expectations is unwise and unfair.

Most of what follows is bleeding obvious, but needs saying. One of the biggest barriers to being able to recognise who you want to employ is the fact that people get very nervous on interview day. You can only see them at their best and, consequently, have the best possible chance of selecting the right person, if they are as relaxed as they can possibly be. If you are leading the day, you need to go out of your way to help them feel comfortable.

The introductory meeting

- Meet them first thing and provide a glass of water, already poured, rather than tea or coffee, which can be a faff to sort and adds to the tension.
- Break the tension and cause a smile by surfacing and apologising for the fact that days like these are barbaric, in that you have to spend all day making small talk with the other people competing for the job.

- Have a detailed plan of the day which is supported by student guides to help the candidates get to the right place at the right time, every time.
- Go through the plan and explain that there will be no tricks, and that they will not, suddenly, be asked to take an assembly to an empty hall at no notice (something I have heard happen more than once) or something similar.
- Allow plenty of time for them to orientate themselves with where they will be teaching, ensuring that they have everything they need for their lesson.
- Acknowledge that teaching a lesson to a class they have never met, in an unfamiliar room, where they have little or no knowledge of the rules of the behaviour system, in front of two people who will decide whether they get the job, are not the best conditions for demonstrating the quality of their practice, and that all you can hope to gain from the process is a sense of what they know about the subject, how they interact with children, how they sequence learning and whether they have the confidence to reshape a lesson in reaction to their ongoing assessment of the students' learning.
- Explain that you will give unvarnished but constructive feedback to them should they be unsuccessful so that they have a better chance of getting their next job.
- Finish the opening chat by pointing out that it is utterly possible, and has been achieved countless times, for a candidate to not be given the job but to enjoy the day.

The tasks

Getting the person specification right, so that you are very clear about what you are looking for in a candidate, is key. Once you have done that, then designing activities to assess the competencies you deem important is the next step. We obsess about four things, which seem to me to be the essentials of being a teacher in a state school today: subject knowledge; the ability to forge good working relationships with students; resilience; and the acceptance of the professional obligation to improve your practice.

Subject knowledge is key. I would argue that there are some subjects where it is increasingly difficult to find subject experts, and so we have to be realistic about the level of academic expertise we can expect in fields for computer science or mathematics posts, for instance. One consultant told me that his MAT had given up giving computer science candidates A level questions at interview because none of the candidates could complete them. And one of my worst appointments had a first class Cambridge degree, whilst one of my best barely met the minimum academic requirements. Yet, I would argue that we must resist lowering our academic expectations of teachers, even if the government's response to the recruitment crisis in schools is to do the opposite.

So, testing candidates' subject expertise is important, especially since degree classifications have inflated so dramatically over the past two decades. For a mathematics post, we set an A level task, which involves candidates giving feedback on a student's wrong answer, followed by a chance for the candidates to explain how they would teach a certain mathematics topic:

TASK 1

Find the exact value of $\int_2^6 \dfrac{2}{x+3}\, dx$

Below is a student's response to the above question.

$$\int_2^6 \frac{2}{x+3}\, dx = \int_2^6 2\,(x+3)^{-1}\, dx$$

$$= \left[\frac{2}{2}(x+3)^{-2}\right]_2^6$$

$$= \left[\frac{1}{(x+3)^2}\right]_2^6$$

$$= \frac{1}{81} - \frac{1}{25} = \frac{-56}{2025}$$

What advice/feedback would you give this student in order to help them progress?

TASK 2

The question below is taken from a Core 4 (OCR) past paper examination. It is worth 6 marks. Design a mark scheme in the space allocated, clearly outlining where each mark will be gained.

3   The equation of a curve is $y = e^{2x} \cos x$. Find $\dfrac{dy}{dx}$ and hence find the coordinates of any stationary points for which $-\pi \leqslant x \leqslant \pi$. Give your answers correct to 3 significant figures.   [6]

The ability to forge good working relationships with students is best exemplified in the classroom. It is usually clear within minutes whether a teacher can communicate well with young people. And the students know within minutes, if not seconds, whether the person in front of them has the humanity to make a great teacher (Pullan, 2019). When I observe an interview lesson, I always try to do as much as I can to enable the teacher to teach. I ensure that every class has name labels, which the usual class teacher gives out at the beginning of the lesson. I frown and glare at anyone who dares misbehave. I even help distribute handouts. I do all of this so that the candidate can relax and teach. I can then get a real sense of how well they can forge positive working relationships with young people; it is an aptitude we also highlight on our reference *pro forma*, but seeing candidates working live with children is hard to beat.

Resilience is an essential trait for all teachers. I have said many times before that we are not mining coal, or performing life-threatening surgery, or diffusing IEDs in Afghanistan, but teaching absolutely is a job that requires the resilience to perform for five hours a day in front of a not always appreciative audience. As Mary Kennedy says so brilliantly, teachers...

> *Portray curriculum content in a way that renders it comprehensible to naïve minds;*
> *For students who are not necessarily interested in learning;*
> *And whose grasp of the content is not readily visible to the teacher;*
> *And who are restless and easily distracted;*
> *In a way that satisfies the teachers' personal needs.*
>
> **(Kennedy, 2016)**

That is a tough gig. Resilience is a key characteristic of anyone who works in schools. So, how do you test for it? Well, beyond the current employer's reference, at the final panel interview we ask the simple question: 'Please could you tell us about an example from the past year where you have had to show significant resilience in your professional life?' We use evidence-based questioning where at all possible. Answers to this question are often probed further, depending upon the quality of the first response. One thing we try very hard not to do on the day of the interview is to make the day of the interview a test of the candidates' resilience itself!

The candidates' acceptance of the professional obligation to improve their practice is a non-negotiable for me. I test that out at interview in two ways. Firstly, I make it clear it is a condition of working at Huntington. I tell the candidates at the very beginning of the day that if they cannot accept such an obligation, then they should go home now. I say it with a smile, but they know I mean it. And then I ask two questions, the first of which has two parts and goes something like this: 'Please could you tell us about an occasion in the last year when you have deliberately implemented a new teaching strategy and it has had a positive impact upon your students' outcomes? (WAIT) How do you know it had a positive impact upon your students' outcomes?' The second question sounds fairly innocuous, but gets to the heart of deliberate practice: 'Please could you tell us about an aspect of your teaching you are currently working to improve?'

Recruiting is an inexact science. The best final panel interviews become conversations, and that can only happen if you, as the interviewer, are expert in your knowledge of teaching and learning and the interviewee feels safe. And ensuring both those things are within your gift. All too often, people ask questions that veer away from teaching and learning. All too often, school leaders take perverse pleasure in making interview candidates feel uncomfortable.

Finally, when it comes to recruiting, it is worth remembering the joy of the job. Geoff Barton once wrote a piece about reclaiming 'the career of teaching for what it can be', remembering to value 'the arts, the sport, the modern foreign languages, the extra-curricular experiences that will help our young human beings to become ever more distinctively human' (Barton, 2018). Geoff's rallying cry is no flimsy, liberal nonsense; the essence of what Geoff says is at the heart of the solution to the recruitment crisis. If we, as school leaders, cannot make teaching an attractive, deeply satisfying, joyful job where the needs of employees – who are our most precious resource – are put first, then our children will never have in front of them the high quality teachers they deserve.

STAFF FIRST BLUEPRINT: RECRUITMENT

- Go out of your way to put your candidates at ease from the outset and never set interview tasks with the aim of catching candidates out.
- Be completely explicit about what you expect of anyone you employ.
- Do all you can to help the candidates when they are teaching.
- Testing your candidates' subject expertise during the interview is essential.
- *Never* appoint if you are unsure about the candidate, despite the thought that 'there will be no one else out there'; that way madness lies.

Part II - Train

The only thing worse than training your employees and having them leave is not training them and having them stay. **Henry Ford**

2. Focus on the early career years
Jonny Uttley

People go into teaching for all sorts of reasons and every teacher has a different story. One of my colleagues, Vicky, who is one of the most exceptional teachers I know, has a story that is very well known across our trust, a story very much in the 'born to teach' vein. From the age of six, Vicky had a well-equipped schoolroom at home. Her class was made up of her younger siblings, and she taught them a range of subjects. This went on for many years, and throughout her childhood she never deviated from her ambition to teach. Once she entered a real classroom, she quickly became an effective and committed English teacher who was promoted rapidly to Head of English and then Trust Director of English. She is now a brilliant deputy head.

If there is a spectrum, then I am at the opposite end. Rather than being born to teach, I suppose I am an accidental teacher. Teaching was never on my radar. Instead of a schoolroom at home, I had my own Old Trafford and my own Lords in the garden. My dreams were of playing in goal for Manchester United or playing cricket for England. After graduating, I was completely clueless and stumbled into a PhD in political science at Syracuse University in upstate New York. It took only a matter of days there before I realised I didn't actually want to do that, and it was really the combination of the need to give my mum an excuse for sacking off the postgrad dream in America and a full-on heart-to-heart with my best American friend in an Irish bar in Washington DC that led me to conclude that a Postgraduate Certificate in Education (PGCE) in history was the best bet for my future! As teachers go, I'm about as accidental as it gets!

In 1997, I started my PGCE at the University of Leeds. When I look back now, I can see my training was as haphazard and accidental as my own decision to enter the profession. Don't get me wrong; I loved my training year. Being taught by the extraordinarily passionate and inspiring Bob Unwin (or Uncle Bob, as we all knew him), my placement with the most supportive and kind colleagues in the history department at Knottingley High School, and teaching the bright and ever-surprising young people of a proud mining community are all things that shaped me as an early teacher and will live with me forever.

The only thing was, I don't think I was really taught anything much about the process of learning, and I was rarely asked to reflect on the effectiveness of my lessons or why some things might have worked and others might not. My Newly Qualified Teacher year at St Peter's School in Huntingdon continued in similar vein. I worked with sparklingly good colleagues, taught great young people and had very little training. In my Recently Qualified Teacher year, I moved into my first promoted post and once again had no training in preparation. None of this is to criticise anyone I worked or trained with. It is simply an illustration of the experience of training and early continuing professional development (CPD) for me and many of my peers 20 years ago.

It is perhaps the lack of high quality, joined-up training in my early career years that has led me to accept and, I am sorry to say, deliver some really poor training. I have sat, listened to and believed a presenter who explained the difference between right-brained and left-brained people. I have stood in front of staff and talked with a straight face and a heart full of conviction about learning to learn. I am not a completely naïve lost cause, though, as I have turned down multiple opportunities to spend a lot of taxpayers' money travelling to America to be trained in the ways of Kagan!

As high quality early career training was never exemplified for me, I have come late to understand its importance and to comprehend the damaging effect its absence has. In the next chapter, we show how to prioritise teacher learning in a highly effective way, but here we argue that we need to prioritise high quality early career development that links the Initial Teacher Education (ITE), Newly Qualified Teacher (NQT) and Recently Qualified Teacher (RQT) years.

The absence of this has been a hugely significant barrier to improving our schools. In *The Teacher Gap*, Becky Allen and Sam Sims explain Becky's experience five years after my own, mirroring my experience of early career training (Allen & Sims, 2019). Becky felt 'ill-prepared by her training' and that in her first job 'it quickly became clear there was no instruction available as to how to get better as a teacher'. Becky, like so many others, quit the profession, and teaching's loss became academia and education policy's gain. Allen and Sims go on to assert that the most significant gap in the system is 'the difference between the quality of teachers we currently have, and the quality of teachers we want'.

The loss of teachers in their early career from the profession has helped create a looming crisis for schools. Coupled with the repeated failure to recruit sufficient numbers of ITE trainees in each of the last seven years and the rise in secondary-aged students, we are approaching a perfect storm in which there is a real danger that we simply will not have enough teachers to teach the children in front of us.

Retention rates of early career teachers have fallen considerably in recent years

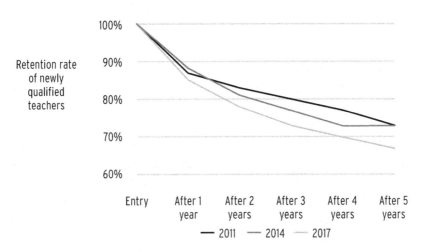

But this is not just about numbers; it is about teacher efficacy and school improvement. A study from Brown University, explained in *The Teacher Gap*, looked at the effectiveness of teachers according to years of experience, and while there are many variables and caveats (notably how often teachers are able to teach the same things in successive years), it shows that 'time in the classroom is a powerful performance enhancer' (Allen & Sims, 2019).

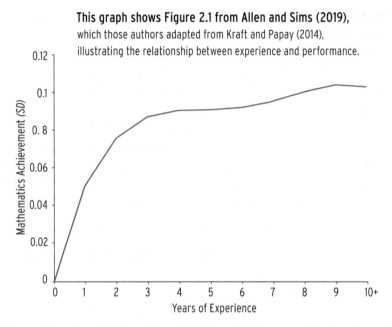

This graph shows Figure 2.1 from Allen and Sims (2019), which those authors adapted from Kraft and Papay (2014), illustrating the relationship between experience and performance.

The problem then is this: we know that the effectiveness of the teacher is the most important factor that we have control over in the success of the student; we know that the rate of loss of early career teachers is increasing and causing a real numbers issue; and now we know that the early career teachers are leaving the profession at the point at which they are becoming most effective.

A system of high quality early career development that underpins a culture of ongoing improvement is at the heart of our blueprint. In a *blueprint school*, having an effective teacher in every classroom will be central to the school's improvement strategy. That cannot be achieved if we fail to develop and retain our early career staff.

Very recent developments give us some cause for hope. In 2018, I was invited to speak at a Department for Education (DfE) event for the regional launch of the Early Career Framework (ECF). I had read the framework quickly without fully processing it, and my initial response was that this seemed like a step in the right direction. Before I spoke, I listened to DfE staff who had been involved in its development and then to Professor Sam Twiselton talking about teacher development. Here were DfE officials, academics and serving school leaders having an informed and honest conversation about the retention crisis, the evidence of its causes and possible solutions. And for the most part, we were all on the same page.

The ECF is a starting point. It is a formal recognition of the significance of years one to three of a teacher's career and the importance of getting training and support right across those years. Many would say the following is better late than never!

> Teachers are the foundation of the education system – there are no great schools without great teachers. Teachers deserve high quality support throughout their careers, particularly in those first years of teaching when the learning curve is steepest. Just as with other esteemed professions like medicine and law, teachers in the first years of their career require high quality, structured support in order to begin the journey towards becoming an expert. During induction, it is essential that early career teachers are able to develop the knowledge, practices and working habits that set them up for a fulfilling and successful career in teaching.
>
> However, too often, new teachers have not enjoyed the support they need to thrive, nor have they had adequate time to devote to their professional development. The Early Career Framework (ECF) underpins an entitlement to a fully-funded, two-year package of structured training and support for early career teachers linked to the best available research evidence. The package of reforms will ensure new teachers have dedicated time set aside to focus on their development.
>
> Our vision is for the ECF to build on high-quality Initial Teacher Training (ITT) and become the cornerstone of a successful career in teaching. (DfE, 2019, p. 4)

The challenge for leaders in *blueprint schools* is how to develop a truly coherent programme of support and development from the ITE year through the early years of a teacher's career. For the last two years, we have been working on this at the Education Alliance. We start from the notion that if we want an effective teacher in every classroom, we need to put structures in place to make that happen. Informing our thinking and underpinning our early career programme is the work that emerged from Sheffield Hallam University as part of the development of the new ITE curriculum. In a literature review published in March 2019, Perry et al. proposed the following working model with three overlapping components:

- learning to teach, including issues such as behaviour management, inclusion, child wellbeing and psychology (both developmental and cognitive);
- learning to teach a subject, including issues of subject knowledge, subject pedagogies, curriculum, children's misconceptions and assessment;
- learning to be a teacher, including issues such as reflection, professional development, working with parents, professional inquiry and understanding of school and educational practices. (Perry et al., 2019)

Although this was proposed for the ITE year, it provides a really simple and effective framework that can provide coherence to a programme of development across the first three years.

Using this framework, we have developed a three-stage model:

Stage One: Pre-training

Our work on developing early career teachers begins before candidates enter our School-Led Initial Teacher Training (SCITT, Yorkshire Wolds Teacher Training). We make school experience available to those who want it and ensure that experience focuses explicitly on each of the three strands outlined by Perry et al. Although most training providers give high quality school experience to candidates in the year prior to joining a SCITT or School Direct programme, we are thinking in the much longer term. We estimate that around 70% of teachers in East Yorkshire schools have either attended East Yorkshire schools as children and/or studied for their degree at a local university. It follows, then, that a large proportion of the new teachers who will join East Yorkshire schools in 2030 are currently students in years 8 to 13 in East Yorkshire schools. So why weren't we engaging with them and developing them as teachers now? Well, now we are!

This year, we held an event attended by 50 sixth form students from across the region who are interested in teaching. They spent a day with us considering what teaching is really about, the different routes into teaching and how they might prepare for a career. We will give them opportunities for work experience and internships in schools and will stay in touch with them over the next few years as they make choices about their futures. Schools have become much better at promoting a range of careers with our young people, but how often do teachers talk up teaching as a great career choice? Schools that put *staff first* will find far more willing advocates for the profession amongst their staff.

Stage Two: Initial Teacher Education

Arguably, the most important organisation with the Education Alliance trust is our SCITT, Yorkshire Wolds Teacher Training. We train between 30 and 40 new teachers each year across primary and secondary and in a range of subjects. Most of our trainees go on to work in schools in East Yorkshire, Hull and York. The programme is built around the three strands of teacher education proposed by Sheffield Hallam. These strands then continue into our NQT and RQT programmes. From the outset, we have thought not just about getting trainees to achieve Qualified Teacher Status (QTS), but how we can set them on the road to a long and sustained career as effective teachers. Running through the SCITT programme are the same *staff first* principles that run through our trust schools.

So we focus heavily on the quality of mentoring, training mentors to the highest level through the teacher educator programmes of the National Association of School-Based Teacher Trainers (NASBTT); we apply the same principles of our trust-wide workload charter to our ITE programme; we tailor each trainee's programme to ensure their level of support is right at all times; and we introduce them from day one to the effective use of evidence. The SCITT was inspected by OFSTED in 2019 and judged to be 'Outstanding' in all areas. The part of the report of which we are most proud says: 'Leaders are clear that they want to develop the next generation of great teachers, ethical school leaders and advocates for the teaching profession. The outcomes for trainees in 2018 and 2019 demonstrate that NQTs have the knowledge and skills to become exceptional teachers'. That all comes from *putting staff first*.

Years one and two of the Education Alliance Early Career Programme

Year 1 - Newly Qualified Teachers

Bringing initial teacher training and early career development into close alignment, so that all newly qualified teachers have access to a shared understanding of how best to develop as a skilful and reflective practitioner.

NQT evidence informed generic pedagogy training

Delivered by Teacher Development Team

 Evidence Informed Practice Project

Engage in thoughtful and enthusiastic discussion about the nature, benefits and challenges of evidence based practice. This will be linked directly to the 3 core CPD sessions.

 A CPD Trust Programme

3 core sessions over the year, including a range of optional twilight sessions that are tailored to suit your needs. Develop best practice in teaching and learning with sessions facilitated by expert practitioners. Optional twilights in behaviour for learning, the working memory and curriculum design.

Chartered College

Teachers in their induction years are funded in their registration for membership of an approved and appropriate professional body. Receive high quality training materials.

A Core Text & NQT Bulletin

Support and enhance understanding of educational research and the teacher standards. See how effective application of both can improve teaching and professional practice.

NQT school specific pedagogy based training

Delivered by School Expert Practitioners

 2 Day Transition

Opportunity to meet other NQTs and get off to the best start. Understand the role and responsibilities of an NQT and the assessment framework. Listen to guest speakers and participate in developmental sessions focused on vision, purpose and workforce well-being.

 School Specific Pedagogy Based Training

Secure foundations and develop best practice by attending school specific sessions on: safeguarding, theory/approaches of assessment, behaviour for learning, SEND code of practice, well-being and pedagogical approaches (modelling/encouraging talk to support learning.)

 Finding the Bright Spots

Facilitated learning walks with ECDL to observe best practice, collaborate with others and reflect on what effective learning looks like.

NQT subject knowledge based training

Delivered by Mentor / Head of Subject / Subject Teacher Development Team

 Subject Knowledge Based Training

Bespoke subject sessions to support personal development needs and interests. Explore subject curriculum intent: the 'why?' and 'what?'. Sessions will steer those new to teaching in understanding the process of curriculum design. This will help teachers ensure learning is broad and balanced, resourceful for all, and prepares our young people for the next stages of their education, employment and lives.

 In-school Support and Positive Psychology Coaching

Develop resilience and maintain good well-being. Have regular meetings with your school mentor, along with additional development opportunities. Timetable reduction in the first year of teaching.

 Managing Workload

Opportunities to address key themes (planning, marking and balancing responsibilities) that may affect workload of teachers in the early stages of their career. Collaborate and understand how to effectively use non-teaching time.

 All underpinned by expert support & fully funded mentor training.

Year 2 - Recently Qualified Teachers

Bringing initial teacher training and early career development into close alignment, so that all early career teachers have access to a shared understanding of how best to develop as a skilful and reflective practitioner.

RQT evidence informed generic pedagogy training

Delivered by Teacher Development Team

 RQT Evidence Informed Introduction to Planning and Implementation

Receive evidence informed training to engage with a project, using a logic model for implementation. Learn from the process of implementation and evaluation, along with developing leadership skills to effectively and strategically drive a subject (Primary RQTs) or project (Secondary RQTs).

 A CPD Trust Programme

3 core sessions over the year to design a project, using an evidenced based logic model for implementation. Engage with and develop understanding of the stages of implementation (Explore, Prepare & Evaluate). Develop leadership skills to strategically drive your project.

Chartered College

Teachers in their induction years are funded in their registration for membership of an approved and appropriate professional body. Receive high quality training materials.

RQT school specific pedagogy based training

Delivered by School Expert Practitioners

 RQT School Project Training

Learn from expert colleagues to develop expertise in a chosen area of interest: subject discipline, pastoral care, SEND provision, mentoring or evidence informed practice.

 RQT Peer Group Sessions

Meet with peers and a specialist mentor to discuss and monitor planned foci to carry out a project. Build effective relationships and share best practice with colleagues to discuss the benefits and challenges of leading a subject or project.

 Finding the Bright Spots

Facilitated learning walks/observations of expert colleagues to develop understanding and awareness of roles and responsibilities outside of the classroom.

RQT subject knowledge based training

Delivered by Head of Subject / Subject Teacher Development Team

 Subject Knowledge Based Training

Revisit and further enhance knowledge of subject curriculum intent. Design and implement your own carefully sequenced subject plan.

 A Core Text

Support and enhance understanding of subject specific pedagogy. See how effective application can enhance subject knowledge and improve teaching.

 Managing Workload

Opportunities to address key themes (planning, marking and balancing responsibilities) that may affect workload of teachers in the early stages of their career. Collaborate and understand how to effectively use non-teaching time.

 All underpinned by expert support & fully funded mentor training.

Stage Three: NQT and RQT years

It is the NQT and RQT years that have proved the Achilles heel of teacher retention. As teacher training has improved, so, slowly, has support and training for NQTs as the transition from trainee to qualified teacher has grown smoother. But what of second year teachers? All too often, this is when the culture shock kicks in. The combination of extra teaching, the removal of mentor support and often taking on responsibilities outside their own classroom has made the second year significantly more challenging than the first year. As the shininess of a new career wears off and the reality of flying solo kicks in, all too many teachers leave.

As part of our school improvement strategy to have a great teacher in every classroom, our trust restructured our central team so that the majority of staff working across schools are in the business of teacher development. As part of that, and with one eye on the emerging ECF, we appointed a Director for Early Career Development. Hayley, the successful candidate, is a highly effective classroom leader with considerable experience of middle leadership and ITE and knowledge of evidence-informed improvement. She has developed a two-year programme, building on the SCITT experience. Over the two years, early career teachers have continued access to high quality mentoring, dedicated non-contact time in the second year, and a well-structured, tailored CPD package that draws on Education Endowment Foundation (EEF) guidance reports and the Research Schools Network.

A *blueprint school* will put having a great teacher in every classroom at the heart of its school improvement strategy. Leaders will understand the crucial importance of the ITE year and the transition through years one and two of a teacher's career. The DfE's ECF provides a structure for support, and while there are problems such as funding and pay that are outside our control, it is for school leaders to do everything we can to halt the loss of teachers from our schools by putting *early career staff first*.

STAFF FIRST BLUEPRINT: EARLY CAREER YEARS

- By putting *staff first*, we create more advocates for teaching as a profession, which will attract more of our current students to become future teachers.
- The first three years (including the ITE year) are crucial to the development and retention of teachers; we should put early career *staff first*.
- A *staff first* approach should begin in the ITE year; whatever is good for qualified teachers is even better for trainees.
- Highly trained mentors and dedicated mentoring time are critical in putting early career *staff first*.
- Invest as much as possible in creating capacity and a structure to support early career staff.

3. Prioritising teacher learning

John Tomsett

When it comes to improving the quality of teaching in your school, it is easy to make token gestures to help you feel like you are doing something. In my first headship, we bought every teacher a copy of Paul Ginnis's tremendous book *The Teacher's Toolkit*. It was a big deal. The book is great if you use it judiciously, over several years, and work on one or two elements of practice you need to improve. Just throwing books at teachers and thinking that is all you need to do will achieve *diddly squat* towards improving teaching. Goodness knows how much that initiative cost us, and goodness knows where those books are now.

Looking back, I don't reckon that gesture of largesse had any impact whatsoever on the quality of teaching and learning. But it made me feel a bit better. I could tell governors that we had bought books and had a whole training session launching the initiative. What I didn't tell governors was that there was no follow-through at all on *The Teacher's Toolkit* initiative, just an after-school launch session. The thing is, I didn't know I was being so rubbish.

I was reminded of my garbage approach to improving teaching when I read Becky Allen and Ben White's seminal post, 'Careering towards a curriculum crash', where the authors articulate at some length the challenge of improving teaching and learning: 'There is no perfect way to reconcile the diverse needs of 30 children in one classroom, in one hour, with one teacher' (Allen and White, 2019). The more you think about teaching a lesson, the more complex the challenge becomes.

To meet the challenge of teaching so that every single student in a class learns, we face an even greater challenge: ensuring that our teachers are active learners. David Weston was close to getting it right when he said, 'If we are going to have more schools where teachers keep improving, we need to [make] staff learning just as much of a priority as student learning'. I say David was close to getting it right, because what we really need to do is put teacher learning *first*, and then, when our teachers become increasingly good teachers, our students will make even better progress.

Improving the quality of teaching across a school is the single most important challenge facing school leaders. It is a tremendously difficult thing to do. When I was first a headteacher, I didn't know what I didn't know about teaching and learning. I was a feather for each wind that blows. I was Dylan Wiliam's magpie, made real - a snapper-up of myriad shiny teaching and learning techniques that one training course after another said would transform examination outcomes overnight.

Too many school leaders want to implement a simple, single, catch-all solution to all teaching and learning ills, whilst the reality of teaching a class of 30 students in a one-hour chunk and getting all of them to make progress is a complex task beyond comprehension. Think about it. Unless you have a class of 15 sets of twins, each student in front of you in period 1 on a Tuesday has had different: experiences since they left school on Monday afternoon; amounts of sleep; breakfasts; conversations with parents/carers/friends/relatives/form tutors; thoughts about the work in front of them we will never get to know; hormones released by their brain; learning experiences since they were born; genome patterns shaping their physiology...you get my meaning. How on earth can we expect to know that every single student in that class of 30 students has made the expected progress at the end of 1 hour of teaching?

As Lee Shulman so beautifully observed, 'After 30 years of doing such work, I have concluded that classroom teaching ... is perhaps the most complex, most challenging, and most demanding, subtle, nuanced, and frightening activity that our species has ever invented ... The only time a physician could possibly encounter a situation of comparable complexity would be in the emergency room of a hospital during or after a natural disaster' (Shulman, 2004). The complexity of teaching can be overwhelming. That may well be the reason why Allen and White's revelatory post is so important. They have addressed the unspeakable. They have pointed out that there is no obvious single intervention that can improve the quality of teaching.

The further problem that can arise from this realisation that teaching in a way that ensures all students learn and make good academic progress is blindingly difficult, or does not exist, is that we admit defeat and give up trying to get better at teaching. Such a stance is so obviously untenable. So, what do we do? The answer lies in improving the quality of teacher learning.

In the last six years, it has become plain to me that the quality of teacher learning is central to putting *staff first*. Any teacher, at any stage of his or her career, must accept, continuously, the professional obligation to improve their teaching. Period. And once the teacher has accepted that obligation, the school must accept the responsibility of providing the very best teacher learning opportunities. School leaders cannot just make a wish that teachers will improve their teaching. School leaders must put their staff's learning needs *first*, before those of the students. It is the most effective way to create an expert teaching team.

So, what does such a professional learning programme look like? First of all, you have to make the time for teachers to improve their practice. Teacher learning time must be woven into the fabric of a school's structure. At Huntington, students go home early on alternate Mondays and we enjoy 2 hours of staff development every fortnight; that aggregates to 38 hours of training time. In addition to that, we provide: 4 training days where most of the 20 hours of time is spent working collaboratively within departments; five 1-hour sessions of a disaggregated training day for curriculum development time; six 1-hour sessions for Subject Leader Training; and five hours of personalised training for classroom practitioners and school leaders to develop their own professional interests. Furthermore, there are tailor-made developmental opportunities for individuals which help them develop specific Sociability-Thinking-Aspiration-Resilience-Knowledge (STARK) aptitudes. That comes to over 70 hours a year of ring-fenced training time for every full-time teacher, as illustrated overleaf.

Any logistical hurdles can be overcome if providing time for staff to work on their practice is genuinely prioritised. Tom Bentley said at a National College of Teaching and Leadership (NCTL) conference in 1996 that 'once you have found your core purpose, change your school's existing structures to accommodate your core purpose rather than contort your core purpose to fit around your existing structures'. If the development of teaching and learning is your prior-

Whole School Training Days: IQ; Metacognition 20 hours	**Pastoral Development & Behaviour Training** 10 hours	**Disaggregated time:** Curriculum development 5 hours
Subject Teaching & Learning Forums 22 hours	**Personalised development training** 5 hours	**Subject Leader development** 6 hours

ity, you *have* to find the hours during the school week for your staff to work on their practice. *No ifs, no buts.* You must not expect them to do it all in their own time. And any logistical barrier can be overcome. Just because half your students come to school on buses does not mean you cannot finish early once a fortnight for training: just sort it out with the bus companies and with your parents. No logistical barrier should stop you improving the quality of teaching. As Fullan says, 'one of the ways to love your employees is by creating the conditions for them to succeed' (Fullan, 2008, p. 25).

Beyond finding the time for teachers to focus upon their learning, you need to ensure that you provide high quality training. If improving the quality of teaching is so difficult, then you need to follow two principles when designing teacher learning opportunities. Firstly, you need to scrutinise diagnostically the impact that current teaching is having upon students' learning in order to identify as well as you possibly can which specific area of practice requires improvement; secondly, you need to turn to educational research to see what the evidence says has the best chance of working within the area of your practice that you have identified warrants improvement.

The cycle of improvement begins with teachers' honest, accurate self-evaluation of their students' outcomes. Indeed, institutional coherence in schools stems from the accurate interpretation of students' performance.

John Jacobs, one of the greatest ever golf coaches, used to say that the best way to interpret what was happening with your golf swing was to study the flight of your ball when you hit a shot. The parallel with teacher improvement is perfect – a forensic analysis of students' results using all the intelligence available is the most important source of evidence for understanding how we need to modify our teaching to improve our students' performance. With the examination boards' online post-results services, combined with our understanding of the combinations of flesh and blood that produced those results, and *copious amounts of our own wisdom and judgement*, we have all that we need to make a decent diagnosis of what needs to be improved in our teaching. The thread from classroom teaching to student outcomes is a golden one; with honest scrutiny, accurate diagnosis can shape the coming year's training focus for individuals, subjects and the whole school.

Once you have a sense of the specific area of teaching you would like to improve, there is an increasingly accessible evidence hoard to support your efforts. The Education Endowment Foundation (EEF) has begun to grow a bank of resources giving a summary of what works best according to research evidence. The EEF Guidance Reports are particularly good, and they include a guide to implementing changes to practice. And there are other good sources of evidence-informed practice from organisations such as the Chartered College of Teaching and Tom Bennett's researchED. For the first time since I trained to be a teacher in 1987, school leaders and teachers have access to educational research evidence. Furthermore, there are experts in the field who can help us translate that evidence base into changes in our teaching that have positive impacts upon students' outcomes.

So, once you have established what you need to improve in your teaching and what the evidence says you might do to help such an improvement, you need people to support you in making that improvement. We would suggest that the leader of teacher learning in school is not the only person who needs to be expert in the field of school improvement. We would argue that every member of the School Leadership Team needs to have a deep understanding of the school curriculum, subject-specific pedagogy, assessment, and how children learn best. Without that knowledge, you do not have the credibility required as a school leader to support colleagues to improve their practice.

When it comes to supporting teacher improvement, there is no one better than Professor Viviane Robinson. Her little-cited but brilliant book *Student-Centred Leadership* centres on my favourite issue: *the golden thread from school leadership to student outcomes*. Robinson's conclusion, having surveyed the research on how leaders make the most meaningful difference in schools, was proverbial music to my ears: *The more leaders focus on their relationships, their work, and their learning on the core business of teaching and learning, the greater will be their influence on student outcomes* (Robinson, 2011). I maintain that headteachers who are really doing their job effectively know this instinctively; what's so great about Robinson's book is that she has the empirical evidence to support this claim.

And when it comes to how to forge the most productive teacher-school leader relationships based on trust, Robinson nails it:

> *You can't be an instructional leader in the sense of leading the quality of teaching ... if you can't have conversations with teachers about the quality of teaching, or the quality of their planning or the quality of their assessment ... [A] lot of instructional leadership gets stuck on the inability to have those conversations ... [T]he challenge of relationships is how to integrate doing the important work with building and maintaining relationships. And people get into trouble when they separate the two out. Integrating the work with the relationship building is critical, because trust is a* result, *it is not a precursor. Teachers trust leaders on the basis of watching them do the work, and how they treat people in doing the work. Teachers don't trust leaders who they don't perceive as competent. The risks I choose to take [as a teacher] to try stuff out is going to depend upon the way the leaders treat me if I fail, so it is a very risky, team-based, interdependent business and that needs trust. [You have to be able to] tackle tough stuff while continuing to build trust.* **(Bastow Institute, 2014)**

So, it is hard to create a culture where teachers are honest with school leaders about the challenges they face in their teaching if the school leaders are not perceived as competent about teaching and learning – what Robinson calls 'the work'.

If school leaders are going to put *staff first*, they need, then, to become experts in teaching and learning. They need to accept the professional obligation to get better themselves, and that obligation can require significant levels of commitment to their own learning. But, in my experience, that is a delight. In 2018, I began giving a talk called '25 years of hurt'. Looking back, my PGCE training was poor. Consequently, I taught for a quarter of a century without really knowing what I was doing – I got by on force of character and sheer enthusiasm. Students enjoyed the lessons. They were engaged. Results were OK, sometimes good, and occasionally excellent. But looking back, it could have been so much better. Only in the last seven years, since I have learnt so much about teaching and learning, have I begun to employ teaching strategies that have the best chance of helping students make good progress in their learning.

My own learning has been self-directed. If you need to improve your own knowledge before you help your colleagues, I would read ten essential publications on teaching and learning. There have been more books on teaching and learning published in the last decade than you can possibly find time to read; however, this admittedly subjective selection will help enormously:

- Harry Fletcher-Wood et al.'s *The Learning Curriculum 2.0*;
- Daniel Willingham's *Why Don't Students Like School?*;
- Dylan Wiliam's *Leadership for Teacher Learning*;
- Viviane Robinson's *Student-Centred Leadership*;
- Graham Nuthall's *The Hidden Lives of Learners*;
- Tom Sherrington's *The Learning Rainforest*;
- Daisy Christodolou's *Making Good Progress?*;
- Mary Myatt's *Gallimaufry to Coherence*;
- Barak Rosenshine's *Principles of Instruction* (or Tom Sherrington's brilliant explanation of the principles);
- Adam Boxer's *Explicit & Direct Instruction*.

As Robinson so convincingly argues, you have to know what you are talking about. And to keep you up to date, there are so many good resources online. People like Tom Sherrington, Harry Fletcher-Wood, Kate Jones, Adam Boxer,

Mary Myatt, Mark Enser, David Didau, Ruth Walker, the Education Endowment Foundation, Alex Quigley, Claire Stoneman, Christine Counsell *and so many more* are publishing their ideas on a daily basis. Over the next decade, there will be new writers. But I do think that these authors are getting to the definitive heart of teaching and learning, and I think new writings will largely be centred upon the key themes of these works.

The thing is, my late-found expertise has helped my mentoring of teachers enormously. As Robinson makes clear, school leaders 'need to be increasingly knowledgeable about the core business of teaching, learning, assessment and curriculum. And they need to be able to use that knowledge to make good decisions' (Robinson, 2018). I performance manage (we actually call it Performance *Development*) 30 members of staff. The Performance Development of our 112 teachers is undertaken solely by our School Leadership Team (SLT). The thing is, what else should school leaders be doing but supporting teachers to improve teaching and learning? What else are those who aren't providing this support so busy doing that is more important?

When leaders support teachers to improve practice, they need to emphasise that they want to see *everyday* lessons. Nothing fancy. No show lessons. Just what we do in our classrooms, day in, day out. Feedback should be swift and dialogic – no judgements, just a discussion about what people think about teaching and why they choose to teach the way they do. Reflect upon what has been learnt and engage in professional conversations and teaching frequently, both formally and informally. But, remember, leaders can only do this if they know what they are talking about.

School structures that have informed leaders of teacher learning and time for teachers to work on improving practice also require coherence with a school's performance management system. A feature of our mature, coherent model of Performance Development and our related CPD programme is our Disciplined Inquiry objective. It is the only objective in our Performance Development. All teachers and teaching assistants – some 120+ colleagues – identify a feature of their practice they would like to develop and then evaluate that development of their practice against its impact upon their students' performance. They are expertly trained in the whole process by colleagues from our Research School who introduce colleagues to, amongst other things, Interventions, Treatment

Groups, Control Groups and Effect Sizes. They have time to complete their Inquiry – we call it their Inquiry Question, or IQ for short – and at the end of the year they write it up on an A3 *pro forma.*

The success is completing the IQ itself, not whether the intervention worked. One of the best IQs of recent years has been in the modern foreign languages (MFL) department, where the whole department explored, in one form or another, the impact of short, regular translation practice upon students' writing skills. It prompted the Subject Leader to contact the University of York languages department, which sent a link to a research paper called 'The Bottleneck of Additional Language Acquisition' (Slabakova, 2018). The MFL department's collective IQ led them to scale up the successful intervention the following year *(for more on the IQ process, please see chapter 5).*

And when it comes to retaining teachers, job satisfaction is key. Job satisfaction grows from individuals finding their jobs purposeful and interesting, with those jobs undertaken in a culture of *challenge* and *trust,* resulting in *successful outcomes* that are *recognised.* It's not just me who thinks keeping the job interesting is important. Andreas Schleicher, Director for Education and Skills at the OECD, claimed in September 2017 that we have to make teaching more 'interesting' and more 'intellectually attractive' if we are going to solve the recruitment crisis (Schleicher, 2017). A key question to answer is how do you keep the job of teaching *interesting*? I recently met with the Subject Leader of MFL and, without betraying confidences, she told me that she loves what she is doing at Huntington because it is 'intellectually interesting'. By creating a school that uses an evidence-informed approach – where research findings complement what we already know from experience – we have done two inextricably linked things: improved our students' outcomes and increased job satisfaction. It has taken a decade to grow a school where trust is deep and genuine, where love has overcome fear, and, now, where we put *staff first.*

STAFF FIRST BLUEPRINT: TEACHER LEARNING

- Focus upon aspects of teaching and learning that have been prioritised diagnostically.
- Underpin teacher learning with research evidence.
- Allocate significant amounts of frequent, regular, ring-fenced pockets of time, which are sustained over time as part of a repeated cycle.
- Make teacher development opportunities multi-layered so that teachers at all stages of their career feel nourished.
- Besides safeguarding, SLT must prioritise teacher learning over everything else that happens in school.

4. Curriculum development
John Tomsett

As I write, at the beginning of the 2020s, curriculum is the educational hot topic. We are living in the world of curriculum 'deep dives'. The curriculum *is* the progression model. Curriculum statements. Subject curriculum reviews. Substantive knowledge. Disciplinary knowledge. Declarative knowledge. Procedural knowledge. Conditional knowledge. The knowledge-rich curriculum. Core knowledge. Hinterland knowledge. The planned curriculum. The enacted curriculum. The assessed curriculum. The learned curriculum. Cultural capital.

The thing is, curriculum development is nothing new. That said, with top-down implementation of things like the key stage 3 (KS3) strategy in 2000, there is a generation or two of mid-career teachers who have never really had to think tremendously hard about curriculum development. For years, they and their school leaders have accepted prescription. When suddenly faced with rising levels of autonomy, schools have found curriculum development demanding.

In a school that puts *staff first*, there are challenges for school leaders when it comes to curriculum development. To begin with, what level of autonomy do you allow teachers in designing the curriculum? People enter the teaching profession for myriad reasons – some because they want to work with children, some because they want to pursue their degree subject, some because they couldn't think of what to do when university finished, some because they tire of the corporate world and want to do something meaningful.

With such a wide range of professional motivation amongst teachers, the variation in curriculum knowledge and understanding is similarly broad. To what extent, then, should teachers decide what is taught? Do we entrust curriculum design to those teachers who do not have a profound understanding of their subject?

There are many current members of mathematics departments, for instance, who do not hold a degree in the subject. To what extent can someone with a grade D at A level contribute to shaping the curriculum? Would you want your child taught A level by someone with a third class degree and three D grades at A level? These are difficult and uncomfortable questions.

We cannot attract sufficient entrants to the profession, so is it wise to raise the academic entrance threshold for prospective new teachers? I once asked an English ITT student who had a third class degree in journalism why she chose to pursue a career in teaching. After saying that she hadn't really thought about that question, she went on to say that she wanted to show to students 'that it wasn't all about being intellectual'. I politely reminded her that, in many ways, it actually *was*. She quit halfway through the year when she found teaching *Pride and Prejudice* to year 12 just too difficult because she had never read it before.

And *there* is the issue, right there in that conversation with the journalism graduate. Virtually all the teachers I have met have wanted to improve the life chances of the disadvantaged. But too many get confused about what that means. The disadvantaged want a choice about the direction of their working lives, and to do that they need a decent set of qualifications. Curriculum then becomes a matter of social justice. Qualifications and knowledge that allow disadvantaged students the choice of entering the professions are challenging. So, do school leaders allow the Subject Leader of PE to decide whether they offer the GCSE or the BTEC at KS4? And once that decision has been made, how does that affect the curriculum in lower school?

When I led Lady Lumley's School in Pickering, we developed links with local businesses, Askham Bryan College near York and the North York Moors National Park. One of our highest flyers decided to choose the countryside and environment BTEC we offered in conjunction with the National Park. That student collected a distinction, along with five A*s in academic GCSEs. All well and good. But attaining only five academic GCSEs meant that if he had wanted to attend, say, Oxford, Cambridge, St Andrew's, Imperial, LSE or Durham, there would have been no point in applying because his application would have been rejected at the first admissions hurdle.

And when we discuss curriculum as a social justice issue, we are making subjective judgements about the worth of different types of qualification and different types of knowledge. One of my students is as sharp as a tack and wants to pursue a career in the law. At the watercooler, he would struggle to converse with any of his colleagues. He would be relatively clueless about current affairs, but he knows what a line bite is when you are carp fishing.

So do we allow my carp fishing student to, metaphorically, carry on carp fishing, or do we give him the challenging qualifications that give him greater choice about his future? It is here that Christine Counsell's views resonate loudly: 'A curriculum exists to change the pupil, to give the pupil new power. One acid test for a curriculum is whether it enables lower-attaining or disadvantaged pupils to clamber in to the discourse and practices of educated people, so that they gain the powers of the powerful.' If you are driven by a moral purpose based around equity, then let him enjoy his angling, for sure, but also get him to focus hard upon the angles in his trigonometry. Give him the *cultural capital* that broadens his *cultural mobility* and enables him to be *socially mobile*. Then he will be able to converse with fishers and barristers alike.

So there are different types of knowledge, which we value differently; the intellectual arguments are both perilous and fascinating. There are subject experts who are revelling in the current debates surrounding the school curriculum. People like Christine Counsell are leading the discussions about what should and should not be taught. There is, however, a huge gap between people like Christine and the vast majority of England's 480,000 teachers. Younger teachers who see teaching as a lifelong career in which they get geekily engrossed are in the tiny minority. Few teachers have the motivation to become deeply engaged in curriculum development; even fewer have the time. The increase in workload in developing curriculum materials at every key stage in England has been significant. Yet, if you dictate to teachers what they teach and provide them with all the materials, you'd be surprised just how strongly many would object to such an imposition.

And then there is the issue of comprehending subject-specific pedagogy, a key element of curriculum design. It is worth asking anyone who teaches: 'What are the specific hallmarks of pedagogy in your subject?' It is a question that initially stumps most people. General responses, such as 'modelling', are not really specific – most subject teachers use modelling techniques as part of their pedagogic armoury. If someone offers 'modelling' in answer to my question, I then ask, 'But what modelling technique is specific to the subject content you are teaching and how does that modelling technique you use in your subject differ from how another colleague teaching a different subject might use modelling as a pedagogic tool?' This follow-up question stumps most colleagues.

To be fair, 'What are the specific hallmarks of pedagogy in your subject?' is a really hard question to answer, but it is crucial that colleagues in each department have a shared understanding of subject-specific pedagogy so that when they plan lessons – particularly for vulnerable students – they do so in a way that addresses the more complex barriers to learning that the subject content inherently contains.

Whilst it is somewhat dated and perhaps flawed, Shulman identifies what he calls 'pedagogical content knowledge', which he defines thus:

> *Within the category of pedagogical content knowledge I include, for the most regularly taught topics in one's subject area, the most useful forms of representation of those ideas, the most powerful analogies, illustrations, examples, explanations, and demonstrations – in a word, the ways of representing and formulating the subject that make it comprehensible to others ... [It] also includes an understanding of what makes the learning of specific concepts easy or difficult: the conceptions and preconceptions that students of different ages and backgrounds bring with them to the learning.* **(Shulman, 1986)**

Shulman's definition is best exemplified by imagining an experienced teacher co-planning with an NQT. The experienced teacher will be able to identify at what point in the lesson students will misconceive what is being taught; the NQT will not. I am a pseudo mathematics teacher. I have one way of teaching simultaneous equations and I find it hard to comprehend why students cannot understand how to solve simultaneous equations after I have explained a worked example. When they ask me to go over it again, I repeat the same explanation, but talk more slowly and loudly, as though I am explaining in English to a garage mechanic in rural France, for the second time, that my car is overheating.

I watched a brilliant mathematics teacher once ask a low prior attaining year 11 class for the answer to this sum: 3t − t = ? It is obviously 2t. Surely no one can get that wrong! The first student he asked for an answer replied: 3t − t = 3. I was gobsmacked. I had never imagined such an answer because, with a grade A at A level, I had always been in mathematics classes with equally good mathematicians. But suddenly I could see the utter logic of 3 as an answer. Knowing those misconceptions will occur so that you prepare an explanation for the students that helps them understand why their thinking is flawed is the hallmark of the teacher who grasps the specific pedagogy of their subject.

So, when it comes to thinking about subject-specific pedagogy, we might begin to move from the generic to the specific pedagogy of our subject by starting with a list of generic techniques, but thinking about how they are specific for our subject considering our subject's specific content:

- Modelling in [subject X] looks like...
- Writing in [subject X] looks like...
- Questioning in [subject X] looks like...
- Exam craft in [subject X] looks like...
- Metacognition in [subject X] looks like...; and so on.

And beyond subject-specific pedagogy, we need to consider the relationship between curriculum content, pedagogy and assessment. In his review of the National Curriculum in 2010, Tim Oates explained why Michael Gove had made so many changes to schools simultaneously:

The term 'coherence' does not carry the meaning typically associated with a 'broad and balanced curriculum' but is a highly precise technical term: a national curriculum should have content arranged in an order which is securely based in evidence associated with age-related progression, and all elements of the system (content, assessment, pedagogy, teacher training, teaching materials, incentives and drivers etc.) should all line up and act in a concerted way to deliver public goods. **(Oates, 2010)**

Oates's claim about the interconnectedness of the curriculum's content-pedagogy-assessment triumvirate can be explained by considering the humble sonnet poetic form. If *one* of the purposes of education is to introduce our children to 'the best that has been thought and said', then I believe that *all students should know and understand the dynamics of the sonnet as a poetic form and how the form has evolved over the centuries.*
  If I were to design a scheme for teaching the sonnet…

- I would want students to know and understand the main sonnet forms – Petrarchan, Spenserian and Shakespearean – and how the sonnet has been developed beyond those definitive forms.
- I would want the students to know the historical contexts within which the sonnet form developed.
- I would want students to know and understand the following in order to appreciate the dynamics of the sonnet's poetic form:

  - key vocabulary central to the sonnet form: octave, sestet, quatrain, rhyming couplet;
  - iambic pentameter;
  - the role of the *volta*;
  - the different rhyme schemes and how to notate rhyme;
  - why poets use rhyme and the impact of rhyme and its relationship to a poem's meaning.

- I would want students to be able to write a critical analysis of a sonnet, using a good range of literary criticism terms.
- I would want the students to learn a sonnet by heart.
- I would want students to write their own sonnets.
- I would introduce a number of sonnets to the students:

- ○ 'In what bright realm, what sphere of radiant thought' - Petrarch
- ○ 'Whoso list to hunt' - Wyatt
- ○ 'On his blindness' - Milton
- ○ 'What guile is this' - Spenser
- ○ Sonnet 18 and Sonnet 130 - Shakespeare
- ○ 'Ozymandias' - Shelley
- ○ 'How do I love thee?' - Browning
- ○ 'Anthem for Doomed Youth' - Owen
- ○ 'Clearances, III' - Heaney
- ○ 'Prayer' - Carol Ann Duffy
- ○ 'I am very bothered' - Simon Armitage

So, how are curriculum, assessment and teaching and learning so inextricably linked? Well, students need to be taught some core knowledge before they can understand the concept of a sonnet (*curriculum content*). I could, for instance, give students a deliberately chosen range of sonnets that exemplify the different forms within the form, and let students work in pairs to identify similarities and differences. They could classify the different sonnets and find there are three main forms with some oddities. I could then tell them directly what the three main forms are called, illustrate the forms with new examples, and label for the students the elements of each form that make them distinctive. Or I could teach *all* that directly from the front (two different approaches to *teaching*).

I could then check, using a whiteboard quiz, to see if the students had learnt how to identify the different forms - I show a sonnet on the board and they write down Petrarchan, Shakespearean or Spenserian or other - an exercise that also reinforces correct spellings (checking *learning* through *formative assessment*). The mode of *formative assessment* depends upon the *taught curriculum content* I want to check has been *learnt*.

What I teach next depends upon the outcome of my formative assessment; if the students have not learnt what I have taught them, I will have to go back and teach the content in a different way. To embed the learning, I could begin each lesson with a new sonnet, read the sonnet, and challenge the students to identify which of the main sonnet forms it belongs to. And I will revisit this content anyway because, as Nuthall claims, 80% of students will have moved new knowledge and understanding from their short-term to long-term memories if they have encountered that knowledge at least three times (my A level students know the Nuthall *3 times* claim better than they know the economics content I am supposed to have taught them...) (Nuthall, 2007).

Weeks later, after I had taught and formatively assessed all the knowledge and understanding I have detailed above (as well as teaching the students the rigours of how to write a literary criticism essay), the summative assessment - the destination towards which we were always heading - would be something challenging like this:

> Read the following sonnets: Shakespeare's 'Sonnet 130'; Spenser's 'What guile is this' ; Petrarch's 'In what bright realm, what sphere of radiant thought'; Owen's 'Anthem for Doomed Youth' and Duffy's 'Prayer'. Choose two of the sonnets and compare and contrast how the poets use the sonnet form to communicate their ideas and feelings.

This essay would *summatively* assess the extent to which the students *know and understand the dynamics of the sonnet as a poetic form and how the form has evolved over the centuries.* Over time, as different cohorts of students have been assessed, I would be able to modify the assessment according to its validity and reliability.

Without knowledge, you cannot develop students' analytical skills. How can they analyse sonnets and write their own without knowing about Petrarch, Spenser, Shakespeare, et al.? Once you have chosen all of the content of the curriculum, chunked that content up into learnable gobbets so that students can cope with manageable cognitive loads, taught that content, and assessed whether they have learnt that content, then they can analyse and evaluate, for instance, 'Memento', a poem I wrote for my sister after she passed away, and decide what features of a sonnet I have used, which I have ignored, and how the content of the sonnet relates to the formal choices I made when composing the poem.

Memento
for Bev

You stood, alert, at deep square leg,
white shirt, blue top, short pleated skirt.
A batter's 'thwack' rang round the rec
and off you flew - *kingfisher blur* -
eyes fixed upon the Stoolball ball
which smacked into your fearless hands
and stuck. Not once, but five more times
you caught the opposition out -
the last, at dusk, to clinch the match.
Dubbed 'Sticky Fingers' by the team,
you won a jet-black, plastic shield
with 'CATCHES' simply scribed in gold;
no bigger than your palm, you hand
it me, to hold when you have gone.

Note: Stoolball is a sport that dates back to at least the 15th century,
originating in Sussex. Traditionally it was played by milkmaids who used
their milking stools as a 'wicket'.

So, you cannot decide *how to teach* until you know the *curriculum content*
you are teaching, and you cannot know whether your students have *learnt*
the curriculum content you have taught them until you have *assessed* their
learning...*all simply inextricable!*

For teachers faced with ensuring that there is coherence between curriculum
content, pedagogy and assessment, school leaders can put *staff first* when
developing a new curriculum by doing the following things to support colleagues:

- Set up a Curriculum Development Group (CDG) comprising middle
  leaders and led by the middle leader who has the greatest
  expertise and is most likely to be trusted by their peers to
  orchestrate the work;

- Remind colleagues that we have been developing our curriculum for years - constantly build upon what you have already, like painting the Forth Road Bridge;
- Give a generous time frame for curriculum review - five years for a complete overhaul is reasonable;
- Provide time for expert training of middle leaders on curriculum development during CDG meetings;
- Insist that all members of SLT are trained in curriculum development and work alongside the subject leaders they line manage when they are reviewing their subjects' curricula;
- Ensure that curriculum development work is privileged on training days and at subject meetings;
- Seek expert support if required - especially in niche subjects like computer science;
- Stress that the debate about the curriculum is central to curriculum development - there is no off-the-shelf quick fix to developing a challenging curriculum for your students;
- Fund membership of subject associations, which extend the curriculum conversation beyond the confines of your school or MAT;
- Encourage teachers to join local subject-based curriculum groups and give them time to attend meetings;
- Emphasise that the National Curriculum is the starting point upon which any individual school curriculum should be based - we are not starting from scratch;
- Encourage curriculum development that has local colour; living in York is a gift for any history teacher and I know one school which begins Year 7 with a tourist bus ride around the city for the whole year group;
- Emphasise the role of the school's values and core purpose in shaping the curriculum;
- Stress repeatedly that any curriculum development is not about pleasing the regulator but is about providing a challenging curriculum for all our students.

And when reviewing the curriculum, begin with the issue you want to resolve. Once that is identified, instead of immediately deciding what to do about the issue, go to the end of the process and describe the change in students' learning you would like to see. Then go back to the problem and decide upon the change required to secure the improvement in students' learning you have identified and outlined. Once you are clear about the curriculum change you want to make, devise implementation activities to ensure that the change is realised successfully, with students' learning improving. Lastly, identify the outcomes of those implementation activities. Building implementation into formulation is crucial to successful curriculum change. Sometimes those implementation activities are incredibly prosaic, as this example illustrates:

Step 1	CURRICULUM ISSUE	The year 7 English curriculum is not meeting the needs of our highest starting students and is not developing all students' foundational knowledge.
Step 3	CHANGE REQUIRED	We are going to swap the current novel *Holes* for *Robinson Crusoe* from September 2021.
Step 4	IMPLEMENTATION ACTIVITIES	Jane to have 2 days off TT to shape materials for teaching *Robinson Crusoe* to mixed attainment classes and Jim will co-write the SoL on day 3.
Step 5	IMPLEMENTATION OUTCOMES	A scheme of learning that is pitched high, has a low floor, is challenging for all, and is well-resourced and easily accessible on the departmental e-folder.
Step 2	STUDENT OUTCOMES	Year 7 students of all starting points will know: the narrative of *Robinson Crusoe*; its socio-economic context; its place as the 'first English novel', etc.

So, to conclude, when it comes to designing the curriculum, the school that puts *staff first* has to love the ones they're with! But that comes with a caveat, expressed concisely by Alex Quigley when he wrote: 'If we don't face head-on the significant challenge of teacher development, then our exciting curriculum debates and plans will come to nought' (Quigley, 2020). That is why we have committed so much of this book to explaining how we develop teachers. It is why it's entitled *Putting Staff First*.

Ultimately, busy teachers are relatively happy to be provided with materials they can tweak to make their own and to have some input into what is taught.

And they like to be led, so the curriculum leaders are key in developing the curriculum in a *staff first* school. A superb blog post by a Minnesotan teacher takes my point further. Jon Gustafson argues that three things work when it comes to supporting teachers to develop the curriculum and associated resources:

- Teachers adopt new resources that are manageable;
- Teachers are more open to resources that incrementally build on prior expertise;
- Teachers are more open to resources that directly address context-specific needs.

He finishes by pointing out that '[i]f a teacher is struggling with ... new curricula or feeling anxious about a new resource, that should be a cue to *listen more and judge less*', surely a mantra for any school that puts *staff first*.

STAFF FIRST BLUEPRINT: CURRICULUM DEVELOPMENT

In *blueprint schools*, staff ask the following questions as a basic starting point for reviewing any aspect of the curriculum:

- What do you want a student to know, understand and be able to apply at the end of year 2/6/9/11/13?
- How do you then plan to ensure that they get to that point, planning with enough looseness to explore 'hinterland' learning opportunities as they arise?
- How do you build in assessment opportunities to ensure that you know whether your students are learning what you are teaching?
- What 'space' is there for you to change your teaching of the content in response to what your formative assessments are telling you?
- What are the subject-specific elements of your pedagogy which ensure that you teach your curriculum content to avoid students' common misconceptions?

5. Towards an evidence-informed profession

John Tomsett

When I hear a school has launched an ***Action-Research-Project-For-All*** initiative, a tiny corner of my soul shrivels and dies.

My wife is an assistant director of Sixth Form. She runs, amongst a host of other things, a highly successful UCAS (Universities and Colleges Admissions Service) system. She has a heavy teaching load, with A level classes in two subjects. We have two sons and I am a headteacher. She leads a busy life.

She came home after work one day in mid-September a couple of years ago and slammed a document down on the kitchen table. 'I've got all this UCAS stuff on and now I've got to do a f***ing action research project.' I commiserated. The guidance was wafer thin. It seemed that the motivation behind the initiative was little more than her school felt it was 'a good thing to do'. At that time, such initiatives were flavour of the month in the CPD world.

Putting *staff first* means removing everything from the staff's workload that does not help them do a better job. When it comes to the futility of completing action research projects, there is nothing better than Ben Goldacre's keynote speech at the inaugural researchED conference at Dulwich College in 2013. He was excoriating:

> *Teachers will describe a research project they have poured their heart and soul into, pretty much alone, in their classroom, that has taken every weekend and most of their holidays, and is methodologically...*

crap! And they have drenched sweat into this, and that is really depressing and really unnecessary.

Years later, Goldacre's words resonate as loudly as ever.

Unless they are pursuing a PhD in their own time, teachers are not researchers; rather, putting *staff first* means we have to create structures where teachers can become better teachers through engaging with research evidence. As a *Research School*, we do not undertake our own research; we leave educational research to educational research teams in higher education institutions. What we do is try to mobilise evidence so that classroom practice is evidence informed and its impact is evaluated.

Having busy teachers trying to undertake their own research is a complete waste of time. So why, at Huntington, do we propose that teachers complete what appears to be an action research project as part of their Performance Development process? Well, the roots of our initiative lie in Dylan Wiliam's researchED conference 2014 talk entitled, 'Why teaching isn't - and probably never will be - a research-based profession (and why that's a good thing)'.

Wiliam concluded that the contribution teachers could make to help the profession become more evidence informed, rather than research based, was both limited and gradated:

All teachers should be seeking to improve their practice through a process of 'disciplined inquiry':

- Some may wish to share their work with others;
- Some may wish to write their work up for publication;
- Some may wish to pursue research degrees;
- Some may even wish to undertake research.

It follows that at a school like Huntington, which is a Research School and where every teacher has accepted the professional obligation to improve their practice, we should follow Wiliam's advice and insist that every teacher should undertake a disciplined inquiry that aims to improve their teaching. Making the disciplined inquiry part of the Performance Development (Management) process, by making it the only objective, ensures 100% compliance. Linking the disciplined inquiry to pay progression may feel like a stick rather than a carrot, but providing the support structures for teachers to complete their inquiry means that the process is a true learning experience and intellectually interesting. Pursuing your Inquiry Question (IQ) *really does matter* at Huntington. We are a school where we put *staff learning first*.

The initial root of the IQ process lies in the analysis of the summer's examination results, at both individual teacher and subject-wide levels. Colleagues get a good sense of where to direct their attention by combining sent-for scripts, question level analysis (QLA), examiners' reports, and what is known of the students' work prior to the examinations. It might be poor performance on extended writing answers, or certain mathematical concepts, or an inability to recall content. Whatever it is, it can be addressed on individual teacher level or more broadly across all the teachers of an individual subject.

The key of the IQ process is to keep the end in mind. The whole point of the inquiry is for teachers to try to answer a question about an area of their teaching and/or their students' learning that appears as though it could be improved. They are changing an element of their teaching and then evaluating the impact of that change.

So, what do those IQ support structures look like? Well, the IQ process moves from identifying the question about a teacher's practice they want answering to evaluating the impact of their intervention. What follows is an account of the year-long training programme that supports teachers to complete their inquiry in a manner that ensures they become deliberate practitioners and that the outcome of their inquiry progresses them as a teacher-learner. The process is a huge investment in teachers and a manifestation of our determination to put *staff first*.

September: IQ training session 1

The IQ process is launched to the whole teaching staff, including teaching assistants, in mid-September. The training is delivered by members of the SLT to the subject departments they line manage. We make it clear that the completion of the IQ process is the single Performance Development objective. We stress that we are not researchers. We explain that we want colleagues to understand that 'deliberate practice' means weighing up what works and identifying the tweaks to pedagogy that are the 'best bets' for improving student performance. And therein lies a key point about defining effective teaching. We use Rob Coe et al.'s definition of effective teaching as 'that which leads to improved student achievement using outcomes that matter to their future success.' According to them:

> Defining effective teaching is not easy. The research keeps coming back to this critical point: student progress is the yardstick by which teacher quality should be assessed. Ultimately, for a judgement about whether teaching is effective, to be seen as trustworthy it must be checked against the progress being made by students.

It follows that evaluating teaching against student progress is essential.

It is crucial that school leaders consider evidence relating to student progress with wisdom and judgement. We highlight the importance of planning the evaluation right at the beginning of the IQ process.

We explain that disciplined practitioner inquiry should lead to deep transformative learning that significantly informs and influences professionals' knowledge and practice, and subsequently has impact upon the students' experience in the classroom. Disciplined inquiry helps us to challenge our assumptions, view our practice through a new lens, and make informed decisions about our practice using the available evidence.

Before going into the detail, we give an overview of the first stages of the IQ process:

- Diagnose the issues in your classroom.
- What is the Outcome with which the intervention will be measured?
- What is the Context?
- Who are the participants and what is the setting?
- Research an intervention that meets the needs of your Outcome.
- Decide how long the duration of the intervention is [EEF guidance states that interventions should be three months or longer].
- Plan the intervention, thinking carefully about how you measure the Outcome using pre- and post-intervention testing.

Beginning, then, with the diagnosis, we pose a set of key questions:

1. Does your monitoring and tracking of student performance and progress over time identify any key issues?
2. Have you identified any skills gap for students within your subject? This could be gaps in literacy skills or memory retention issues, for example.
3. When comparing progress between different groups of students, have you identified any anomalies or possible areas for development?
4. Can you identify low achievement or underachievement for students in different classes/topics? Are there any surprise results you may want to focus on?
5. What is the hardest or most challenging aspect of your subject? Are there difficult elements of the curriculum you want to tackle in terms of further support for specific group(s) of students?

Once those questions have been considered within subject areas, we introduce the structure of the IQ itself. This is key to ensuring that the IQ process has the best chance of being undertaken in a disciplined manner:

What impact does **[what practice?]** delivered over **[how long?]** have on **[what outcome?]** for **[whom?]**?

The specificity is key and is stressed throughout the training.

At the end of this first session, we set a gap-task. We ask departmental colleagues to complete, collectively, a subject-specific 'potential areas of inquiry' document, where they sketch out possible lines of inquiry.

We ask them to make some preliminary plans about whether they are going to work as a department, a teaching team or individually. Collaborative approaches, where a number of teachers are working on a single line of inquiry, are often very effective.

The support structures are crucial. If we are putting *staff first*, we have to invest time and resources. As had been stated already, we cannot just *wish* our teachers to get better.

Huntington School
Professional Development

DEPARTMENT:

1. *Articulate your department priorities to your team*
Department Priority:

Whole School Focus: To deliver the Teachers' Promise to our Vulnerable Students

Key learning from delivering Promise:	**Key learning from exam analysis:**
What has your department learnt from focusing on Our Promise with the vulnerable learners over the last academic year?	What priorities have been identified from your exam analysis?

2. *Discuss the possibilities for your department's Inquiry focus*

Remember the focus should be rooted in your department and whole school priorities.
The key question for focusing the inquiry is: What is important, and therefore worth spending time on, given where our students are at?

3. *Explore teaching strategies that underpin the department focus*

If your department priority is on developing deeper knowledge and understanding for vulnerable learners, you could, for example, as a department, focus on recall strategies, with IQs based on spaced practice, interleaving, quizzing, etc.

4. *Seek further guidance*

Which topics would you benefit from further resources on? Do you have any further questions or require any additional support?

Department IQ focus:

October: IQ training session 2

The gap-task completed, colleagues arrive at the second session aware of the area of practice they want to develop. We now provide them with access to the relevant evidence base.

Easy access to evidence findings is key. Here is Ben Goldacre again, back in 2013, addressing the researchED conference delegates:

> *Research gets made and then it just kind of sits there. Research is no good if it is [just] published in an academic journal. Research only matters if it gets put into practice, if it gets used by you to change what you do for the good of children and also yourselves. That is the only way research becomes meaningful. And so we need, desperately, to have clear structures for disseminating the results of research to practitioners, to the foot soldiers, to the people at the coalface. And that can take many forms. Sometimes it can be academic journals, but, good grief, I mean, most doctors can barely be bothered to read academic journals ... everybody who is a member of the British Medical Association gets the British Medical Journal delivered to their door and the conversation you see the most about this, as they pile up in the toilet, is, 'Do I take off the plastic wrapper before I put it in the recycling box or is it OK to stick the whole pile in?' So, what you need is clear three-paragraph summaries of research that are meaningful and relevant to you, which say, 'What did they do?', 'What did they find?', 'What are the strengths and weaknesses of that research, and what needs to be done next to resolve the outstanding uncertainties about what works best?'*

So, the aim of this second session is to provide colleagues with sources of research evidence that they can use to shape the intervention at the heart of their IQ. We give them an *Evidence-Based Reading pro forma* to record their findings, with detailed prompts for enhancing their thinking as they browse the evidence we have collated for them:

Huntington School
Professional Development

Evidence-Based Reading

DEPARTMENT:

DEPARTMENT FOCUS:

1. *My area(s) of interest*

2. *What do I already know and what do I need to find out about to inform the planning of my question?*

   If you are continuing along a line of Inquiry, what did you find last year? What did teaching our vulnerables tell you?

3. *What were the article(s) you read? Summarise the salient points in bullet points below.*

4. *How does the research help inform the planning of your Inquiry Question?*

5. *What are your initial ideas about your question (e.g. working groups, classes, controls)?*

Next steps: Choose your write-up format preference; craft a first draft question & start writing up your 'ingredients'. Next session: December XX during the Teaching & Learning Forum.

Huntington School
Professional Development

What student cohort have I identified for the intervention and why?

Some considerations:

- **How small or large is my student cohort?** In terms of delivering successful classroom interventions, small is good, although the more students you have the more individual anomalies you can discount in your results.
- **Does the student cohort span across different ages, ability ranges, teaching classes, etc. and how much does this matter to the efficacy of the results?** Typically, the narrower or clearer the focus, the more variables you can discount.
- **Am I selecting a 'treatment' and 'control group' from my student cohort?**
- **Is the process of student cohort selection 'randomised' or 'matched'?** 'Cherry picking' students is an instinctive cheat we can commit!
- **Is the intervention going to be known or hidden from my students?** 'Blinding' an intervention (for both teachers and students) can remove unwanted variables.

What Pre- and Post-test will give me the most useful results?

Some considerations:

- **Do I have a quantitative assessment that is reliable and that synchronises well with the impact of the intervention?** Different test types will provide relative strengths and weaknesses.
- **Do I have any qualitative assessments that can support my quantitative assessment?** Student self-reporting is less reliable than testing, but useful in different ways and often provides a very useful 'process evaluation'.
- **Are my assessments practical and manageable?** Does the assessment form part of 'business as usual', or is more effort required?
- **Do I have enough data to triangulate my assessment data?** It is ideal – but not always achievable – to have more data points.

What are the limitations and obstacles that affect my inquiry?

Some considerations:

- **What methods will reduce the number of variables that limit my ability to prove that the intervention had an impact?**
  - *Having a realistic time frame;*
  - *Having peer support to co-plan and devise a reliable trial;*
  - *Matching cohorts;*
  - *Matching teachers, e.g. co-planning; same amount of time, etc.;*
  - *Having multiple assessments (within reason);*
  - *Creating more objectivity, e.g. peer marking.*

What are the results of my inquiry and how generalisable are they?

Some considerations:

- **Do the results fit an expected hypothesis?** If so, why? If not, why not?
- **What limitations and obstacles should make us cautious about interpreting the data?**
- **What should we stop doing as a result of the 'disciplined inquiry'?**
- **Are the results generalisable across student cohorts, different teachers, different subject domains, etc.?**
- **Is there a case for doing nothing as a result of the 'disciplined inquiry'?** *If so, what have we learnt from the process evaluation?*
- **What should we change as a result of the 'disciplined inquiry'?** If so, *what have we learnt from the process evaluation?*

We explain the hierarchy of evidence, from the most robust to the least:

Indicative strength	Type of evidence
80%	Meta-analysis or systematic review: analysis and summary across many individual evaluations
70%	Matched-comparison design or Randomised Controlled Trial (RCT): tests intervention against a randomly chosen comparison group
60%	Sound theory backed by a growing body of empirical research, and may cite DfE policy/White Paper.
40%	Independent research/evaluation: uses surveys, data analysis, monitoring, interviews, observations, focus groups, etc.
15%	Internal/in-house evaluation. Not independently evaluated: includes case studies, observation, interviews, etc.
15%	Expert opinion/advice from consultants, academic or sector group
10%	Media articles/anecdotal reports and interest groups

We stress to colleagues that they should always seek a high standard of evidence. Meta-analyses use a statistical approach to combine the results from multiple studies in an effort to increase validity over individual studies, and to improve estimates of the size of the effect and/or to resolve uncertainty when reports disagree. One might argue that it may be misleading to describe meta-analyses as the "gold standard", however; in general, of course they are, but not always. A recent study (Kvarven et al 2020) found that effect sizes in meta-analyses were on average three times the size of those in pre-registered multi-site replication studies, which are, arguably, the best guide to what we could expect in real settings. A single RCT with a good fit to the IQ could be a far better guide than a meta-analysis of a broad area.

We explain that self-sourced evidence is acceptable, but that they should always check against this recommended hierarchy of validity for robustness. Other evidence from wider reading/research/subject area should not be dismissed as it may be appropriate for the identified area of inquiry.

Other sources of independent research our colleagues are directed to include:

- subject-specific or topic-specific blogs;
- subject associations;
- the Education Endowment Foundation (EEF) Toolkit;
- EEF Promising Projects;
- EEF Guidance Reports.

Importantly, we establish an electronic resource bank of evidence, collated by both subject and topic area, in our Research Summaries folder:

Name
► #Research Summaries
► Behaviour and confidence
► Careers, Aspirations and Work
► CPD
► Evidence-based practice. Must read su...
► Extended learning
► Formative assessment
► Gender
► Growth mindset and GRIT
► IRIS
► Literacy
► Literacy across the curriculum
► Mathematics
► Memory and metacognition
► Mental health
► Mental toughness
► Metacognition
► Mindset – Confidence – Resilience
► Parental engagement
► Recall, Quizzing, Self-testing
► Spacing and interleaving
► Student grouping
► Student motivation
► Student questionnaires
► Subject-specific documents
► Using TAs effectively
► Vocabulary and communication

We give colleagues an hour in subject areas to sift through the research summaries and to discuss with each other what area of practice they might work on. They begin completing their Evidence-Based Reading *pro forma*.

The time for discussion is important. Such professional collaboration is both developmental and reassuring. Indeed, Philippa Cordingley is quite clear about what the evidence says about conditions for effective teacher learning, which include (from Cordingley, 2013, with minor adaptations):

- the enabling of sustained peer support and reciprocal vulnerability, which increases ownership, commitment, and a willingness to take risks, unlearn established assumptions and habits, and develop new understandings and practices;
- modelling of this kind of deep and sustained, enquiry-oriented learning by school leaders who provide time for collaborative analysis and evidence-based reflection and who specifically encourage risk taking.

Our IQ process is deliberately woven through with precisely the features of effective teacher learning advocated by Cordingley.

Before the end of the session, we introduce colleagues to the two different formats – A3 or A4 – for writing up their findings. Again, these are easy to access, easy to use and, importantly, pithy.

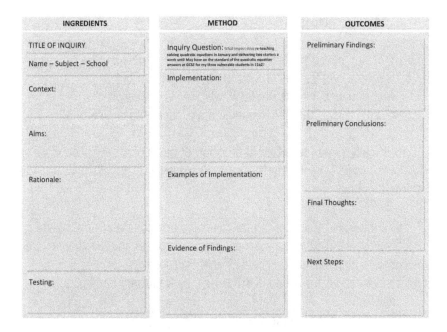

The gap-tasks to complete before the next training session are as follows:

- Access the research evidence and complete the Evidence-Based Reading *pro forma*;
- Choose the IQ write-up format document;
- Create a first draft inquiry question.

December: IQ training session 3

The third session is primarily concerned with finalising the wording of the IQ itself. We re-present the model for crafting effective IQs derived from the EEF guidance, which helps colleagues maintain a targeted, specific approach:

What impact does **[what practice?]** delivered **[over how long?]** have on **[what outcome?]** for **[whom?]**?

This should encompass:

- [what practice?] = The INTERVENTION being evaluated;
- [over how long?] = The DURATION of the intervention;
- [what outcome?] = The OUTCOME which will be measured;
- [whom?] = The CONTEXT, including the participants and setting.

Once they have an idea of an IQ question or questions, they need to be as specific as possible. Vague questions can be a barrier to successful evaluation. We urge them to:

- be clear about the intended outcome and how they want to measure it;
- be clear about what approaches they want to test and the changes that need to be made in order to deliver them properly;
- be clear about the group of students they want their findings to apply to;
- involve colleagues in the discussion.

Now that colleagues have an idea/outline for a question, we need to check/guard against a flawed question. Here are three possible questions that are listed in order of effectiveness:

1. How can we improve our Science GCSE results?
2. How effective is **Multiple Choice Quizzing** in **improving knowledge retention** in **year 11 science classes**?
3. How effective is **Multiple Choice Quizzing once a week for 12 weeks** in **improving knowledge retention in science** for **year 11 low starters**?

Question 1 is way too vague. It is as though there has been no analysis of student outcomes whatsoever, other than, perhaps, the realisation that the examination results were poor.

Question 2 lacks a specific time frame for the intervention and is not specific with regards to a cohort of students.

Question 3 meets all the criteria for an effective IQ. The teacher might have been even more specific about the science content they wanted the students to know.

Here are examples of highly effective IQs:

- 'How does targeted teaching (24 x 10-minute sessions over 12 weeks) of tier 2 vocabulary impact on increasing the use of tier 2 vocabulary in extended writing for low-starter boys in 7X2?'
- 'What impact does increasing the frequency of modelling writing, followed by structured metacognitive reflection in lessons delivered January to June, have on the quality of creative writing for my low-starter students in 10X4?'
- 'What impact does explicitly teaching Tier 2 and 3 geographical vocabulary using knowledge organisers, delivered over two terms, have on the appropriate use of tier 2/3 vocabulary in written responses for the SEND students in my Y8 class?'

Shaping the IQ is probably the most important guidance point during these first three sessions of training. It is worth noting that we do not rush the process. The spring and summer terms are set aside for implementing the intervention.

But before colleagues are sent off to implement their intervention, there is further preparation work required. The third session asks this question: 'What is most likely to get in the way of you doing your IQ?' The most common issue can be 'remembering' the IQ process in a busy schedule, so a task for the remainder of this session is to populate the timeline we provide with key dates/actions/moments for completing the IQ.

We also ask colleagues to think about what may stop them from successfully implementing their IQ – not if it will be a success, but rather what might get in the way of them completing it. We ask them to complete what we term a *pre-mortem task*, where they anticipate what might cause failure so that they can address it, rather than reflecting on failure the following September via a *post-mortem*!

Lastly, we explain how they might evaluate the impact of their IQ. We ask them to begin the evaluation before they begin the intervention. To help them, we urge colleagues to take seriously the establishment of a baseline to evaluate against, as this baseline informs what they go on to do. We suggest there is a huge choice about the data they can collect to establish their baseline:

- Attainment;
- Year-on-year data or previous cohorts of a similar type;
- Matched comparison; if comparing two classes, then use a selection of high-starter, mid-starter and low-starter students, as well as our more vulnerable students;
- Attendance;
- Behaviour/engagement;
- Questionnaires:
  - Pre-existing?
  - One you write?
- Interviews (Students? Teachers? Support staff?);
- Reading ages;
- Lesson/small group observations;
- Student work;
- Student voice;
- Teacher voice.

There may be other sources. We suggest that they might combine two or three sources of data and ensure a mix of quantitative and qualitative data.

We also suggest that they are realistic when it comes to gathering data. It is key that the IQ does not become a burden. Collecting hoards of data for the sake of it only adds to workload and is unnecessary.

A comparative group or control group is advised but not always possible, which is fine. This may require some 'joined-up thinking', but may be more possible with a collaborative approach within departments or by working in sub-groups. At its most basic, organising a comparative or control group is summarised in this graphic, which uses the same measures at pre- and post-intervention test, but with only the intervention group experiencing the intervention:

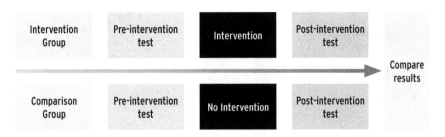

The best comparison group would be one where the teacher has randomly chosen the students, which would eliminate any teacher bias during the selection process; however, randomisation can be difficult, and it is not essential if we are operating as deliberate practitioners rather than researchers.

When thinking around baseline testing, we ask colleagues to work back from how they intend to know if a change in practice has worked. The most common methods of intervention measurement at Huntington School are listed below:

- assessment scores before and after the change made to practice;
- example of student work before and after;
- student/staff questionnaires before and after;
- student interviews before and after;
- observation/IRIS review before and after.

We warn colleagues that using generalised outcomes such as GCSE results can be difficult in terms of isolating the many factors that may or may not have seen a change to performance in a public examination. Our guidance is:

- Be as precise as possible, for example, question level analysis around a particular Assessment Objective is more valid and useful - importantly, incorporating this into an IQ is not adding additional testing/workload to the process;
- Qualitative data is very powerful - for example, 'before' and 'after' student work that shows the desired change in student action. Remember we are deliberate practitioners, changing aspects of our teaching approach, not researchers. We are undertaking a process of disciplined inquiry.

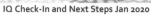

Huntington School
Professional Development

IQ Check-In and Next Steps Jan 2020

Inquiry Question:

Summarise in one sentence *WHY* you have chosen this focus

Whole School Focus: To deliver the Teachers' Promise to our Vulnerable Students

Where are you up to? Use the checklist questions to prompt your response:	**Thinking & Planning Checklist, have you...?**
	☐ Determined the intervention
	☐ Chosen a cohort
	☐ Identified a control group
	☐ Planned the duration, frequency and timing of delivery
	☐ Prepared a pre-test
	☐ Collected pre-test data
	☐ Prepared the resources necessary for the delivery of the intervention
	☐ Planned a post-test
Next Steps? Use the checklist questions to prompt your response:	**Thinking & Planning Checklist, have you...?**
	☐ Used the timeline to plot when you will complete the actions listed above
	☐ Chosen the format for the write-up of your IQ and started to complete the document
	☐ Contacted your PD reviewer with when they might be able to see your IQ in action in lessons or TLF

Huntington Research School

For the bulk of the session, colleagues work on refining their IQ. We are there to provide advice as part of an IQ clinic.

By the end of the autumn term, we have trained colleagues on a number of aspects of disciplined practice that derive from research protocols, but the overall process does not constitute educational research. Our classroom practitioners have begun the process of becoming deliberate practitioners. Our final message before colleagues begin implementing the IQ intervention is this: 'The process of completing the Inquiry is the objective, rather than whether or not the intervention is successful...'

January: IQ training session 4

Further time is set aside on the training day in January for departments to work on the final planning of their IQ. The key now is to ensure that colleagues are clear about what to do regarding the faithful *implementation* of their IQ. We provide another *pro forma* to help them shape their thinking so that any barriers they might have to undertaking their IQ are minimised.

After that, and during the implementation and evaluation phases, line managers/PD reviewers are invited to share in the process, whether that is seeing the intervention live or during IQ reflection sessions in department Teaching and Learning Forums (TLFs). There is an expectation to involve the SLT Performance Development reviewers so the IQ becomes a tangible process and less of an abstract evaluation when we reach the end of the annual cycle in September.

The IQ is monitored through regular conversations between teachers, subject leaders and Performance Development reviewers. Any lesson observations that form part of the PD process will usually focus upon the IQ.

The IQ is written up after the summer's examination results. Significant time is given to teachers in early September to evaluate their IQ intervention, including QLA from the examination board websites.

An example of a successfully completed IQ

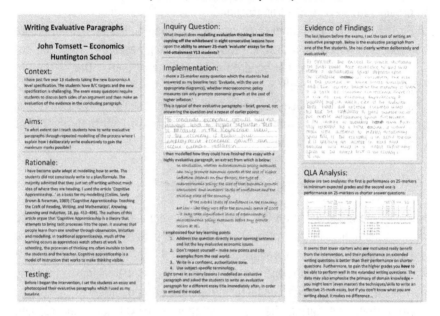

Writing Evaluative Paragraphs
John Tomsett - Economics

Context

I have just five year 13 students taking the new Economics A level specification. The students have B/C targets and the new specification is challenging. The exam essay questions require students to discuss both sides of an argument and then make an evaluation of the evidence in the concluding paragraph.

Aims

To what extent can I teach students how to write evaluative paragraphs through repeated modelling of the process where I explain how I deliberately write evaluatively to gain the maximum marks possible?

Rationale

I have become quite adept at modelling how to write. The students did not consciously write to a plan/formula. The majority admitted that they just set off writing without much idea of where they are heading. I used the article, 'Cognitive Apprenticeship: Teaching the Craft of Reading, Writing, and Mathematics', as a basis for my modelling (Collins, Seely Brown & Newman, 1989). The authors of that article argue that:

Cognitive Apprenticeship is a theory that attempts to bring tacit processes into the open. It assumes that people learn from one another through observation, imitation and modelling. In traditional apprenticeship, much of the learning occurs as apprentices watch others at work. In schooling, the processes of thinking are often invisible to both the students and the teacher. Cognitive apprenticeship is a model of instruction that works to make thinking visible.

Testing

Before I began the intervention, I set the students an essay and photocopied their evaluative paragraphs which I used as my baseline.

Inquiry Question

What impact does **modelling evaluation thinking in real time copying off the whiteboard** in **eight consecutive lessons** have upon the **ability to answer 25-mark 'evaluate'** essays for **five mid-attainment Y13 students**?

Implementation

I chose as my baseline test a 25-marker essay question which the students had answered: 'Evaluate, with the use of appropriate diagram(s), whether macroeconomic policy measures can only promote economic growth at the cost of higher inflation.'

This is typical of their evaluative paragraphs – brief, general, not answering the question and a repeat of earlier points:

> To conclude, economic growth will not always lead to higher inflation. This is because, in the Keynesian view, if the economy is below full employment economic growth can occur without inflation.

I then modelled how they could have finished the essay with a highly evaluative paragraph, an extract from which is below:

> *In conclusion, whether macroeconomic policy measures can only promote economic growth at the cost of higher inflation depends on four factors: the type of macroeconomic policy; the size of that economic growth; consumers' and investors' levels of confidence and the existing state of the economy.*
>
> *If the overall levels of confidence in the economy are low - like they were after the economic crash of 2008 - it may take significant levels of expansionary microeconomic policy measures before any growth occurs at all.*

I emphasised four key learning points:

1. Address the question directly in your opening sentence and list the key evaluative economic issues;
2. Don't repeat yourself - make new points and cite examples from the real world;
3. Write in a confident, authoritative tone;
4. Use subject-specific terminology.

Eight times in as many lessons, I modelled an evaluative paragraph and asked the students to write an evaluative paragraph for a different essay title immediately after, in order to embed the model.

Evidence of Findings

The last lesson before the exams, I set the task of writing an evaluative paragraph. Below is the evaluative paragraph from one of the five students. She has clearly written deliberately and evaluatively:

> To conclude, the extent to which increasing the funds banks have available to lend will reverse a deflationary spiral depends upon: the confidence of consumers, the size of the increase in bank funds available and the current state of the economy. If there is a lack of consumer confidence there is a risk of the economy experiencing a liquidity trap, in which, even if the available bank funds did increase consumers would not have the confidence to spend therefore would not reverse deflationary spiral. Furthermore, if the increase of available bank funds only increased by a little amount, it would make little difference to reversing deflationary spiral. Also, if the economy is in such a recession it is unlikely an increase in bank fund available will result in a reverse deflationary spiral as the current state of the economy is so low.

QLA Analysis

Below are two analyses: the first is performance on 25-markers vs minimum expected grades and the second one is performance on 25-markers vs shorter answer questions:

Student		Avg QCA score	Avg GCSE score	Grade	Min. exp. grade
B	M	49.84	6.64	C	B
P	F	49.24	6.54	A	B
G	M	49.00	6.50	A*	B
E	M	48.52	6.42	D	B
H	F	47.20	6.20	B	B/C

Rank order for 25-marker questions (/100):
1. G: 89 (+2 rank order)
2. P: 81 (=)
3. H: 66 (+2)
4. B: 48 (-3)
5. E: 25 (-1)

Student		Avg QCA score	Avg GCSE score	Grade	Min. exp. grade
B	M	49.84	6.64	C	B
P	F	49.24	6.54	A	B
G	M	49.00	6.50	A*	B
E	M	48.52	6.42	D	B
H	F	47.20	6.20	B	B/C

1. G: 89% vs 80% (25-markers vs shorter questions)
2. P: 81% vs 72%
3. H: 66% vs 60%
4. B: 48% vs 70%
5. E: 25% vs 55%

It seems that lower starters who *are* motivated really benefit from the intervention, and their performance on extended writing questions is better than their performance on shorter questions. Furthermore, to gain the higher grades, you *have* to be able to perform well in the extended writing questions. The data may also emphasise the primacy of domain knowledge – you might learn (even master) the techniques/skills to write an effective 25-mark essay, but if you don't know what you are writing about, it makes no difference...

A research-informed profession?

The successfully completed IQ illustrated above is clearly not research; it is merely a disciplined inquiry. That said, the process is thorough and deliberate. It exemplifies Dylan Wiliam's demand that 'all teachers should be seeking to improve their practice through a process of "disciplined inquiry"' (researchED, 2014). It also illustrates the high levels of investment in teachers in a school that tries at every turn to put *staff first*.

Professor Jonathan Sharples once commented to me that what we have created at Huntington is, in his eyes, 'globally unique', in that all our classroom practitioners employ an evidence-informed approach to improving their teaching. Up to a point, he is correct. But we have a long way to go – back to Ben Goldacre and his 2013 researchED address: 'We need to think about what we might achieve in a decade or two, a generation or three; how teachers and researchers can network to find out what works and then to do it.'

To illustrate the scope of the challenge we face in developing an evidence-informed profession, a certain Performance Development annual review meeting sticks in my memory. The colleague in question had taken me through her IQ expertly. She had evaluated the impact of her intervention. From the matched trial she had constructed, the data strongly suggested that her specific intervention had impacted positively upon her students' learning. Later in the meeting, she mentioned another intervention she had used. I asked her what impact this second intervention had had upon her students' learning. She looked at me blankly. 'I don't know', she said. 'I hadn't thought to evaluate it.'

For that teacher, the IQ process was a hoop through which she had jumped in the name of Performance Development. It had not fundamentally changed her approach to her practice. The holy grail of deliberate practice is not just to complete the IQ; it is to change the thought processes of our teachers, so that they become professionals who consciously think about every aspect of their practice and who evaluate the impact on students' learning of what they are doing on a regular, systematic basis. Such teachers would understand at a profound level the fundamentals of an evidence-informed approach to developing teaching and learning. They would be Dylan Wiliam's ultimate in truly deliberate practitioners. But they would not be researchers.

Ben Goldacre wrote in his seminal publication *Building Evidence into Education* (2013) that:

> [W]e recognise that being a good doctor, or teacher, or manager, isn't about robotically following the numerical output of randomised trials; nor is it about ignoring the evidence, and following your hunches and personal experiences instead. We do best, by using the right combination of skills to get the best job done.

And as Arthur Eddington said in 1935, '[o]bservation and theory get on best when they are mixed together, both helping one another in the pursuit of truth.'

I only wish I had invested in my own learning earlier in my career. My PGCE was next to useless. I taught for 25 years and, as I mentioned already, I got by on force of character and enthusiasm. I didn't really know why I was doing what I was doing. I mimicked those who had taught me when I was at school and I borrowed ideas randomly from colleagues. I grew my own repertoire of teaching strategies, which were never really evaluated. It's not that I was a bad teacher, but I think I could have been so much better. It has only been in the twilight of my career that my teaching has become evidence-informed and my classroom practice has, as a result, improved considerably. My reservoir of experience was suddenly enhanced by what I was learning from research evidence. For the first time in my whole career, *I put my own learning first.*

STAFF FIRST BLUEPRINT: EVIDENCE-INFORMED PRACTICE

In *blueprint schools*, teaching will be an evidence-informed practice because a leadership wisdom prevails that creates structures which enable teachers to:

- access good evidence easily;
- feel encouraged and safe to change their practice in the light of the evidence;
- be supported by a school-based research lead with a Higher Education connection;
- feel intellectually interested in the process of improving their teaching;
- evaluate the impact on student outcomes of the changes to their pedagogy.

Part III - RETAIN

Train people well enough so they can leave, treat them well enough so they don't want to. **Richard Branson**

6. Managing workload

Jonny Uttley

One chilly February Friday afternoon, about three years ago, I was standing outside school on gate duty talking to my deputy head. Mitch is an enormously hard-working, dedicated leader with significant responsibility in school and a very busy life outside. I was joking about what a sad old man I have become, with my weekend starting when I arrive at the supermarket to buy the Friday night ready meals. I turn my emails off my phone in the supermarket car park and don't turn them back on until Sunday. Mitch looked at me, slightly quizzically, and said, 'Oh, wow! Can I do that?'

In mid-October of the following academic year, I had the sense that some of the staff in school were frazzled and a bit grumpy. The optimism of the new school year had worn off, the nights were getting longer, the marking load was increasing, students were getting tired, and half-term was still that bit too far away. But there was something else going on; the performance management deadline was approaching, the frenzy of lesson observation and review meetings was in full swing. My Director of Mathematics, Matt, was particularly hard hit. He was fitting in eight lesson observations and leading eight end-of-cycle reviews, each lasting about an hour. That was 12 hours that Matt spent seeing and hearing about things he already knew.

Matt is an exceptional subject leader, and over the year was in and out of classrooms, talking to staff in groups and individually, coaching, supporting and developing them as teachers. The department had achieved a Progress 8 score that summer of +0.99 and an ALPS 2 at A level, and maths was one of the most popular subjects in school among the students. Looking back now, I don't think anything Matt did in those 12 hours of 'performance management activities' that October had any positive impact on the lives or outcomes of the young people in our school. I wish I could go back and tell him to spend six of the hours planning lessons and the other six with his young family.

The point of the first story is that the amount of work teachers are expected to do has become all consuming; the point of the second is that our issue with workload is that it is not just about the volume of work, but the type of work and the number of things teachers are asked to do in schools that no longer pass any test of common sense.

Almost everyone who works in a school knows we have a system-wide workload crisis. The 2018 TALIS (Teaching and Learning International Survey) report showed that, despite four years of focus on workload by the DfE and unions, both secondary and primary teachers reported that they were working more hours than in 2013, and the proportion of secondary teachers describing their workload as 'unmanageable' had risen from 51% in 2013 to 59% in 2018.

There is compelling evidence that volume of work is driving teachers from the profession. In its 2019 survey of 8,000 teachers, the National Education Union (NEU) found that 18% of teachers expect to have left the profession within two years, and 40% of teachers expect to have left within five years. Of those indicating the intention to leave, 62% cited workload as the main reason. Given that teachers are both the best and worst advocates for our profession, it is likely that the workload issue is also discouraging new entrants from joining; after all, you are likely to think twice if the teacher you talk to about the profession is one of the 40% looking to leave.

Teachers' working experience is fuelling a shortage of teachers, and this, in turn, is causing the greatest barrier we face in improving our schools - putting an effective, engaged and happy teacher in every classroom in our schools. In their book *The Teacher Gap*, Prof Becky Allen and Sam Sims summarise extensive evidence that shows that, of all the features of a school, the quality of teacher has by far the greatest impact on a student's achievements. They quote Eric Hanushek from Stanford University, who says that '[n]o other attributes of schools comes close' (Hanushek, 2010). So tackling workload is more than just about recruiting and retaining great teachers; it should be at the heart of any school improvement strategy.

But we argue that it goes even beyond that: for us, it is a moral and ethical problem too. How much longer can we hold on to the notion that it is okay for us, as public servants, to ask teachers to make the choice between being a 'good' teacher and being a good father or mother or sister or husband or son or friend? And if the price of great results for children in one school is that the children of the teachers in that school missed out on years of Saturdays or Sundays with their mum or dad, is that a price we should really ask people to pay?

There is a great deal a headteacher or CEO of a MAT can do to improve colleagues' work-home balance, but it must be a high priority and needs real engagement. Over a period of 18 months, we worked with our union county reps to develop a 'Workload Charter' for staff across all our schools. We began by asking the unions to table every issue they wanted to discuss. These included marking, meetings, emails, written lesson plans, 'mocksteds' (mock inspections in preparation for Ofsted inspections) and data inputting.

Nothing the unions asked to discuss was unreasonable, and we made significant progress through honest dialogue and the application of common sense. One of the most interesting discussions was around emails outside work hours. There are lots of interesting and seemingly innovative ideas around email, including switching the system off in the early evening or delaying sending until the next day. But when you take time to think through the implications of these ideas, they create as many problems as they solve.

For example, if a colleague wants to leave school at 3:30 p.m. to pick up their children, do tea, CBeebies, bath time and bed before making the choice to read and respond to emails later in the evening, that is a perfectly appropriate professional decision to make. A school that turns off the email system, say, at 5 p.m., removes that professional decision from the teacher and may well lead them to stay in school longer to 'finish off'. It was through face-to-face dialogue that we were able to explore a whole range of grey areas and acknowledge that tackling workload is not simple, straightforward or something that is ever 'done'.

The product of this work is the trust-wide Workload Charter. It addresses every area the unions asked us to consider, but goes far beyond. The charter speaks for itself and is a live document that we review and seek to improve continually. As CEO, I meet directly with staff to discuss their day-to-day experience and to get feedback on what more we might do. Workload is a regular agenda item at union meetings, trust board meetings and SLT meetings. Staff perception of workload is a reportable key performance indicator (KPI), and in the year in which the charter was launched, the percentage of staff across the trust agreeing that 'the organisation helps me achieve a healthy work-life balance' increased from 59% to 76%.

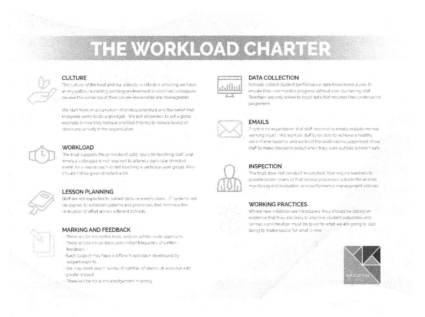

However, the issue of workload is as much about type of work as quantity of work. Ever since I entered the profession in 1998, there has been talk of tasks teachers were required to do that didn't require professional training. More recently, the discussion has been less about administrative tasks and more about burdensome demands that take the teacher away from the core job of teaching and have little impact on improving outcomes - complex data systems, long written reports, individual lesson plans and so on. For us, there remains so much in schools that no longer passes the common sense or the 'Why do we do that?' test.

Often, these things have come about from introducing a new system or process and forgetting to abandon the old one. For example, when performance management was first introduced to schools, most teachers were asked to set three targets, be formally observed, and have an end-of-cycle review meeting. This was when there was little, if any, ongoing quality assurance.

The one-off lesson observation might have been the only time in the year when another colleague came into your room other than to grab some textbooks, and the review meeting was often the only professional conversation you had in the year about what you did in the classroom. Somewhere along the line, we introduced learning walks, paired drop-ins, book checks, discussions with students, coaching conversations, professional learning communities and so on.

The three targets, formal observation, and annual review meetings had been replaced with something better (where it was done in a non-toxic environment); it's just we forgot to stop doing the old system! The result is that thousands of teachers across the country are still spending hours of their time on relatively worthless performance management activities.

Tackling the problem of 'pointless work' can be both transformational and liberating. At a trust planning event, we gave out Post-it notes and asked trust senior leaders to write down anything they can think of in schools that is time consuming but doesn't really improve schools and outcomes for young people. It took an awful lot of Post-it notes! Highlights included setting three performance management targets (why always three?!), long applications for threshold, writing up line management meeting notes, complex marking policies, special pens and stamps for marking, bureaucratic recording of student behaviour, book scrutiny by non-specialists and lots more.

This led to two terms of abandonment in which we tried to root out as much nonsense as possible. Here again, face-to-face meetings are crucial. The headteacher or CEO should sit with staff and invite people to challenge any practice they want to challenge and suggest for abandonment. If anything suggested fails the common sense test, then it needs to go. By opening up a process like this, we can no longer justify a senior leader with a degree in chemistry scrutinising year 11 GCSE Spanish books and feeding back to the MFL teacher (with a Master's degree) on how rapid student progress was.

All this is not enough, though. No amount of workload reduction will keep people in the profession if the culture in which they work is toxic. There is no point in being 30 hours under the stipulated 1,265 hours if a successful graduate professional is visited three times a day by a non-specialist senior leader with a clipboard in their hand and wearing a special jacket. While this may seem facetious, too many teachers still report that they work in a culture of audit and surveillance and low levels of professional trust.

CULTURE

The culture of the trust and our schools is critical in ensuring we have an enjoyable, rewarding working environment in which all colleagues believe the demands of their job are reasonable and manageable. It is essential that our schools are led in an ethical way that is driven by moral purpose. Many of the difficulties that staff experience in schools come from a high stakes accountability system that can drive leaders to behave in ways that increase stress and anxiety for staff. We insist that our leaders do everything they can to guard against this, that they set a good example in how they behave and that they try to reduce levels of stress and anxiety in the organisation. Seeking to reduce the number of tasks staff undertake is likely to have little effect on improving work/home balance if this happens within a toxic culture and an environment of high threat. To support this we offer training and development for our managers and leaders to ensure they are able to translate the vision and values into behaviours which are built on the principles of dignity, respect, professionalism and integrity.

We start from an assumption of professional trust and the belief that everyone seeks to do a good job. Leaders should be clear that processes of monitoring and evaluation and performance development are, for most staff, about recognising great practice and supporting colleagues in their professional commitment to get better at their jobs. They are absolutely not about surveillance and catching people out. In order for this to be a reality, processes must operate within a spirit of openness and transparency and staff must be made to feel confident to raise any concerns or issues they have. Part of the assessment of leaders' performance is the effectiveness with which they contribute to developing a thriving culture of openness, honesty and kindness, in which we make the lives of staff better as well of those of young people.

The most significant part of our Workload Charter is the section we wrote on 'Culture'. This attempts to articulate how we want leaders to act and how we decided to change our systems to reduce anxiety and stress in the organisation. By publishing this, we have committed ourselves as leaders to try to live up to the standards.

None of this is easy. But we believe firmly that it is only in a culture that starts with an assumption of professional trust that we can tackle the deep-seated issues around workload in a way that the various initiatives of the last 15 years have failed to do. We must reduce the volume of work and rebalance the type of work we ask people to undertake. But this will only stick if a core responsibility of leaders is to do everything they can to reduce anxiety and create and protect a culture of openness, honesty and kindness. It is about treating people like people. It is about putting our human *staff first*.

STAFF FIRST BLUEPRINT: MANAGING WORKLOAD

- Teacher workload is about both quantity of work and type of work; improved staff wellbeing is a by-product of managing workload effectively.
- Managing workload must be a top priority for school leaders and should be part of all school planning, quality assurance and reporting processes.
- School leaders' regular and genuine face-to-face engagement with staff is crucial.
- Leaders should seek to reduce the volume of work but also abandon pointless work; do fewer things but do them better.
- The impact of actions to reduce workload should be measured and reported.

7. Getting student behaviour right

Jonny Uttley

If you talk to teachers who have recently left or are thinking about leaving the profession, they generally talk about two issues: workload and behaviour. In Chapter 6, we looked at how we can put *staff first* by tackling workload. Here we consider how we can do the same by getting behaviour right. So much has been written on the subject of behaviour in schools, and it is the subject of daily battles on edu-Twitter. So it is, perhaps, a surprise that this is one of the shortest chapters in the book. However, it is precisely because of the vast literature and regular Twitter spats that we are keeping this short and to a very small number of points.

While we have legitimate and deeply held concerns about practices in a small number of schools with indefensibly high levels of exclusions and exceptional student movement that is explained away as students unwilling to conform to high standards, we have no interest in diving down a rabbit hole that leads nowhere. There are so many debates about labels that are put on ideological positions, and we do not label the approach we advocate in our *blueprint*. We are not 'zero tolerance' or 'warm:strict'; we do not campaign to 'ban booths' and we do not throw stones from the sidelines. We are two school leaders who have led successful schools; we have done many things well and we have made some mistakes. But we both acknowledge grey areas and complexity, and there is little in life more complex than dealing with the behaviour of 1,500 teenagers every day.

At its core, leadership in a *blueprint school* is about identifying and removing barriers so staff can get on with their jobs unencumbered. The question, then, is how can leaders put *staff first* and remove barriers around student behaviour? The Education Endowment Foundation's guidance report on 'Improving Behaviour in Schools' is a good place to start (EEF, 2019). When it was published in June 2019, it was seized upon by both sides in the Twitter spat to prove their case. One side latched on to recommendation five, 'use targeted approaches to meet the needs of individuals in your school', while the other side seized upon recommendation six, 'consistency is key'. Focusing on individual recommendations and ignoring others gets us nowhere. The report needs to be considered properly, with each recommendation examined in the context of all others, and leaders in a *blueprint school* should carefully and honestly consider what barriers exist in their school and how they might be removed.

In the summer of 2018, when Scott took up his role as Head of Driffield School - a school previously in 'Special Measures' - his first priority was to identify what barriers existed for staff in getting behaviour right. He did this by looking at lessons and behaviour around school himself, talking to teaching and non-teaching staff and to students. He then deployed his leadership team to remove those barriers. It was this process that led to the implementation of a new and simple behaviour policy and system based on:

- high profile rewards that all students can access and that promote positivity;
- really clear stepped sanctions, but with each new week starting afresh;
- highly visible SLT who genuinely support staff;
- a centralised detention system so staff don't set their own.

In short, the SLT are asked to do everything they can to allow teachers to get on with what they are really good at - teaching. In January 2020, the school emerged from the shadow of Special Measures when Ofsted judged the school to be 'Good' in all areas. The report says that '[p]upils are happy at the school and say that it feels safe. Pupils behave well and are positive about their school'. We know there is plenty more work to do, but I am absolutely clear that without the SLT prioritising behaviour and supporting staff in genuine and practical ways, we would not have completed this turnaround.

The really important point to emerge is this. Scott did not make the mistake that many incoming headteachers do; he did not change the behaviour policy because it was a 'big ticket item' that needed to be changed to make an impact. He looked for the barriers to good behaviour by listening to staff and collecting as much other information as possible, and then made a small number of clear, implementable changes. It was this process that led to the change in student behaviour. The new system makes it easier for staff to do their difficult job, reduces their workload and has improved their wellbeing. SLT take the lead responsibility for the standard of students' behaviour and, by doing so, they implicitly put *staff first*.

It is hard to argue that a senior leadership team identifying barriers to good behaviour and then taking responsibility for removing those barriers is not a good thing. But it is probably much easier to do at the start of headship or in a school in difficulty than, say, five years into headship in a school that is seen as a good school. Having honest and open discussion about behaviour is one of the very real difficulties in schools, as it seems to be the last taboo of teaching. There is something that cuts to our core as teachers if we feel people think we ever struggle with behaviour. Just ask yourself honestly, would a teacher in your school feel equally comfortable asking these two questions to a colleague or leader?

'I'm struggling to get my year 7s to really grasp the concept of succession to the throne. Any thoughts?'
'There's a small group of students in my year 9 class who are really offside with me and disrupt my lesson. Any thoughts?'

Leaders feel the pressure of the same taboo. If you ever want to knock a headteacher's confidence or provoke a reaction, just say that 'behaviour's really not been great around the place the last couple of weeks, has it?' If a teacher struggles with asking question two and a leader gets triggered by this last question, we are not yet fully there with our *staff first* culture.

As the CEO of a trust that now has six 'Good' or better schools, I am taking a fresh look at behaviour in well-established, successful schools. I am spending time with staff and students in each school and, while my conversations go into some depth, there are essentially only two questions:

- What are the barriers staff face?
- What more can leaders do to remove those barriers?

The EEF guidance report provides a useful framework for this work. Under each of the six recommendations, there are many things leaders in a *blueprint school* will do or will at least consider:

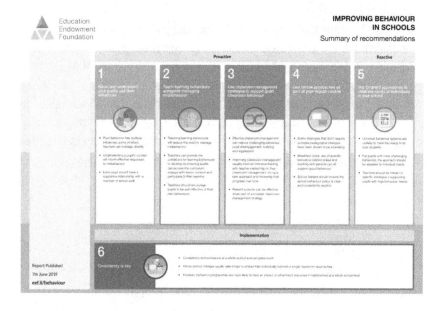

Recommendation one:
Know and understand your pupils and their influences

By removing barriers, reducing anxiety and reducing workload, leaders ensure that staff have time and are in the right frame of mind to get to know students better. Structure tutoring to put a premium on knowing students and their influences. At Driffield School, the new headteacher moved to mixed structure with heads of year responsible for year groups and house leaders working across the age range to ensure all students had a supportive relationship with a member of staff.

Recommendation two:
Teach learning behaviours alongside managing misbehaviour

This is an area where many schools have made less progress. The teaching of learning behaviours has been overlooked in many schools where the prevailing culture has been that students should know how to behave and conform to expectations. This does not help teachers in the classroom and does not fit with a *staff first* approach.

Recommendation three:
Use classroom management strategies
to support good classroom behaviour

Reward systems in all our schools have been redeveloped and made more visible. A recent series of discussions I had with students across all ages revealed key stage 4 students to be as motivated by rewards as key stage 3 students. The most effective behaviour training for staff is through a reflective, coaching model where teachers feel as confident talking openly about behaviour in their classrooms as they are talking about pedagogy. It is only in a genuinely *staff first* culture that this openness is likely to be established.

Recommendation four:
Use simple approaches as part of your regular routine

Classroom routines, particularly around the start and end of lessons, are effective. Atul Gawande's *The Checklist Manifesto* is an excellent treatise on the efficacy of using checklists to gain consistency in fundamental processes within organisations. It is especially applicable to schools, where, like in Huntington, they want 1,700 people to behave in a very precise way several times a day.

Take the start of lessons. Why not train teachers to begin lessons using a checklist like this?

- Have your bell work ready before opening the classroom door.
- Greet each student with a smile and a hello as they come in the door, saying their name.
- Stand at the front, centre of the room, and explain that whilst they are getting on with the bell work, you will be taking the register.
- Take the register promptly, whilst scanning the room and intervening if anyone is off task.
- Walk around the room and check that everyone is ready for learning and that everyone has a planner on their desk.
- Move to the back of the room and debrief on the bell work.
- Move to the front of the room to review the learning from the last lesson and introduce the new learning planned for the coming lesson.

Now, it takes a lot of discipline to make such a checklist translate into teachers' practice. But the effort is definitely worth it. In all the work I have done in schools and with schools in challenging circumstances, when the school moved from a series of ad hoc routines across the school to tighter, standardised routines, behaviour improved and teachers were able to teach more effectively. Tom Sherrington and Doug Lemov have both published superb advice on how to break down such routines into learnable, doable chunks (Sherrington, 2020; Lemov, 2015b). Leaders should support the implementation of new routines and are vital in ensuring that momentum is maintained. This is at times laborious and boring work, but it is a vital part of leadership if we are truly to *put staff first*.

Recommendations five and six:
Use targeted approaches to meet the needs
of individuals in your school/Consistency is key

And so to finish with the Twitter spat and the imagined conflict between 'use targeted approaches to meet the needs of individuals in your school' and 'consistency is key'. In fact, there is no conflict here whatsoever for leaders who want to take a *staff first* approach. Although it is not easy, a successful *blueprint school* will seek to balance these two ideas, and leaders will spend a lot of their time checking the balance and ensuring it is right. In a school that is run with recommendation five to the detriment of recommendation six, a teacher exists in a world of ever-shifting sands. They are unsure of systems and of what is expected of whom. In a school that is run with recommendation six to the detriment of recommendation five, the teacher becomes a cog in a machine that is utterly consistent but lacks compassion and humanity. Relationships with young people are more difficult, and teachers are required to impose a standard that for some young people will never be appropriate. Both approaches create barriers for staff rather than removing them.

Consistency and clarity of systems (both for rewards and sanctions) give staff a safe space in which to operate, knowing they have the backing and support of leaders. Uncertainty and anxiety are reduced, teachers are more confident in their classrooms, and as a result it is easier to establish positive relationships and focus on teaching great lessons. It was consistency that made all the difference to staff at Driffield on the school's journey to recovery. Using targeted approaches for a small number of individuals creates more fairness, not less, and gives teachers the chance to treat all students with decency and common sense. The key to targeting approaches effectively is that leaders should be immersed in this work; it should come from knowing students well and should always be agreed in advance, through a proper process, and it should be recorded. Staff are undermined when an approach is tailored retrospectively or a sanction is changed in response to a complaint.

When it comes to behaviour in schools, every member of staff needs to be consistent. And here's why, encapsulated in a simple anecdote:

> At all our schools, we have banned headphones and earphones. We twigged, way after we should have done, that at the end of the wire of a student's innocent looking head-/earphones is a mobile phone, which is banned at our school.
>
> So, what do you do when you see one of your most law-abiding, compliant students with their earphones just visible – that sneaky white earbud obvious to the naked eye and incontrovertibly seen by you, and the student knows you have seen it, and you know the student knows you have seen it?

Well, you have to confiscate the earphones. Turning a blind eye is not on, no matter how easy it would be for you and the student to tacitly agree that you haven't noticed the transgression.

The key reason for absolutely having to pursue a confiscation is that when your colleagues challenge your most difficult students about the same rule-break, it is ten times easier for them to do so if everyone does. And it's ten times harder if just one member of staff doesn't make that challenge.

Behaviour management is a collective effort. Every time you impose the rules, you are supporting your colleagues and securing the culture of the school. There can be no exceptions.

When it comes to behaviour management in a *blueprint school*, every colleague has to implement the rules on a relentlessly consistent basis. By doing so, they *put each other first*.

STAFF FIRST BLUEPRINT: GETTING STUDENT BEHAVIOUR RIGHT

- Make conversations about behaviour the norm and as valid and important as conversations about curriculum and pedagogy.
- Agree that good behaviour comes from a collective approach and not from a group of isolated teachers working hard on it in their own classroom silos.
- Be clear that leaders are there to remove barriers.
- Do the heavy lifting by centralising as much as possible so teachers can teach.
- Recognise the complexity of balancing consistency and individual need and work continually to check the balance is right.

8. Inspection

John Tomsett & Jonny Uttley

This blueprint is only concerned with what school leaders and teachers have the power to decide about how to run a school. It is primarily about how to ensure that a school's practices are all aimed at helping teachers do their job as well as they possibly can. As Marc Rowland (2019) says: 'Focus on what's in the school's gift. Otherwise we end up chasing the wind.' There is very little we can directly influence about levels of school funding; we can, however, decide how best to undertake lesson observations to improve teacher performance. Every feature of a *blueprint school* puts *staff first*.

That said, as the profession's regulator, Ofsted has an inordinate impact upon the way schools operate. School leaders are understandably prone to shape practice within their schools to meet whatever standards are detailed in the latest Ofsted inspection framework. Our blueprint for preparing for an Ofsted inspection is entirely coherent with our philosophy for running schools: *put staff first*.

Here is a blog post I wrote for Ofsted a couple of years ago, and every single word of it still stands today.[1] It is a *blueprint school's* approach to preparing for an Ofsted inspection:

Surely it is a given that all of us want to be the very best for our students, every lesson, every day. We want to teach solidly good lessons, day in, day out. If we

---

1. Minor format changes have been made to suit the format of this book.

work in a school where everyone is being the best they can be in the classroom every day, every lesson, then that is all we can do.

It follows that we have to do all we can as school leaders to make it as straightforward as possible for our colleagues to teach. We have to remove all the activities that get in the way of teachers teaching well and pay heed to workload. We have to support teachers to follow this process: assess students' work; plan responsively so that teaching is informed by assessment; give students feedback on their work; teach lessons that help students progress in their learning; set student assessments that show how much they know, understand and can apply; assess students' work ...

If we can create schools where this practice is occurring relentlessly, then whether Ofsted is in school or not is irrelevant. You and your colleagues are doing all you can for your students and that is all anyone can ask. As Sir David Carter said to me recently, 'People think that teaching "rock star" lessons is what you need to do to be judged outstanding. I say that teaching consistently good lessons that are well planned and progressing sequentially from the previous lesson is outstanding.'

These are five things you can do that will help your colleagues teach solidly good lessons every day of the week, without adding to their workload:

1. Stop excessive lesson observations and ban making judgements of lessons – instead, ask your teacher colleagues how you can observe them in a way that will best help them to improve their teaching;
2. Ensure meetings finish on time. There should be no prizes for looking busy – work in a way that suits you. Let colleagues go home if they are not teaching last period of the day;
3. When it comes to performance-related pay, begin from the assumption that everybody will get a pay rise unless their students' outcomes are poor, and use your wisdom when making that call, with utter transparency;
4. Embrace a marking and feedback policy designed from the bottom up by classroom practitioners, based upon a set of principles, different according to the subject;

5. Identify one or two key pedagogic priorities for developing over the year, stick to them and provide high quality training for colleagues to support their development.

When it comes to preparing explicitly for an Ofsted inspection, senior colleagues should bear all the burden. All you should ask of your classroom colleagues is to teach as well as they possibly can, which they will be doing anyway, for the students. Your supportive, light-touch quality assurance processes will give you the confidence that solidly good work is going on in classrooms every day.

At the end of school on the day you get the inspection notification call, when you bring your colleagues together, your advice as a senior colleague should be limited to the following:

- Welcome inspectors into your room and be as helpful as possible towards them;
- Make available any information on the students you have and use in your planning;
- Plan solidly good lessons, keeping our development priorities in mind.
- Teach as you have learnt to teach over the past couple of years. No whizz-bang lessons, just plain good teaching and learning;
- Don't be here late; go home as soon as you can and get some sleep;
- Embrace tomorrow and keep things in perspective – what's the worst thing that can happen? Honestly?

Senior colleagues should make sure the following things are in place, all year round:

- A school development plan, which details two or three things you are doing to improve the school, and a review of things that could be stopped or made more efficient;
- A side-of-A3 self-evaluation form, which is updated regularly and 'speaks' to the development plan;
- Good records of performance management processes that minimise the impact on workload;

- A forensic knowledge of the students' genuine progress, especially around the following groups: disadvantaged students, low/mid/ high attainers, and students with SEND [special educational needs and disability];
- A record of what you are doing, with student premium funding, for disadvantaged students, which is different and additional to what you are doing for all students;
- An overview of the curriculum and where you are as a school in reviewing the curriculum;
- A complete, functional, single central record;
- Student portraits where you have intervened to improve the students' progress and the impact has been tangibly positive. Although this is not necessary for an inspection, it helps make tangible what you might claim about your school.

And there are other things, all of which are not difficult for senior colleagues to identify from the Ofsted handbooks, including Ofsted's *myth-busting document*. The key thing is, all of this must be kept from the rest of your colleagues. And all of this should be in existence all of the time if you want your school to be the best it can be at all times for your students.

The bottom line is that the only way school leaders will secure a good outcome from inspection is to ensure that their teacher colleagues can teach as well as possible. And that cannot be achieved overnight. So, as a school leader, don't prepare for Ofsted; instead, create a culture where your teachers can thrive. The best thing for students is a team of highly motivated, well-trained, happy, healthy and expert teachers and support staff. So don't put students first, put *staff first*, because then everyone will better off.

Above all else, look after people. Lead a school where the students' outcomes are almost a by-product of the culture you have established over the years.

The best test of a school is what is going on when no one is looking. Doing what is best for students and staff every lesson, every day, every week, all year, is the best preparation for Ofsted. If you do that, you'll be Ofsted ready every day.

When it was published, I received positive feedback from many quarters. Even our Chief Inspector thought it was 'a very good piece'.

At the Education Alliance Trust, they have gone one further. They have enshrined the refusal to worry about the external regulator in their charter:

INSPECTION

We believe that the best preparation for external inspection is for staff to be able to do the best job they can do, without the additional stress that can be caused by the prospect of the process of inspection. It is the responsibility of the leadership team to prepare the school properly, but this should be done in a way that does not cause significant additional workload for teachers. The trust does not conduct 'mocksteds' that require teachers to provide lesson plans or that involve processes outside the normal monitoring and evaluation and performance management policies. Leaders should be mindful of the messages they send to staff and are asked not to use phrases like 'Ofsted expects to see...' as a matter of course.

STAFF FIRST BLUEPRINT: INSPECTION

- In *blueprint schools*, school leaders know that the best preparation for inspection is to create a culture where their teachers can thrive.
- In preparing for inspection, *blueprint school* leaders bear all the burden; all they ask of their classroom colleagues is that they teach as well as they possibly can.
- In *blueprint schools*, everyone is being the best they can be in the classroom every day, every lesson, and that is all that anyone can do.
- In *blueprint schools*, teaching consistently good lessons that are well planned and progressing sequentially from the previous lesson is outstanding.
- The best test of a school is what's going on when no one's looking.

9. Systematic staff feedback

John Tomsett

I have never worked with a teacher who hasn't wanted to do a good job. It follows, then, that if teachers cannot perform their job well, it is the school's systems that are preventing them. And the quality of the school's systems is the responsibility of the SLT. Ultimately, if a teacher performs badly, it is the responsibility of the headteacher.

This may seem a simplistic argument. There are many variables in a big secondary school over which the headteacher has little control. But the argument is one made best by the American industrialist W. Edwards Deming. In the 1950s and 1960s, Deming's management theories were credited for Japan's two golden decades of growth after World War II. Deming's thinking inspired production systems that made Japan's car industry, for instance, the best in the world.

To illustrate the argument that the leaders of an organisation are responsible for workers' poor performance, Deming used the *Red Bead Game*. In an 11-person role play, 6 colleagues are workers, 2 are counters, 1 is a chief counter and 1 is a recorder. The 11th person, the foreman, is in charge of the game and is the only one who knows the rules.

The 11 are employees of a white bead production company. The foreman has a box of 3,200 white beads. He has a paddle that has 50 bead-size holes. The job of each worker is to put the paddle into the beads, shuffle the paddle under the beads, and remove the paddle four inches above the beads at a 47° angle, shaking off the excess beads so that a white bead is inside each of the holes on the paddle. A successful 'day's work' is a paddle containing 50 white beads.

Before the game begins, the foreman adds 800 'defective' red beads, which are exactly the same size as the white beads, so that the workers know what a defective bead looks like. The system has been designed by the best brains in the business, so it must be perfect. Consequently, workers are not allowed to talk to each other. It has been proven that workers concentrate on their work better if they work in silence.

The foreman declares at the end of day one that the target for each worker is to produce 50 beads per day with one use of the paddle, making it clear that three red beads is the maximum allowed per worker per day. The two counters and the chief counter have *pro formas* on which they note down each worker's daily production, and the recorder has a large board on which to record publicly the workers' daily outputs.

With 20% of the beads red, it is all but impossible to achieve the target of three red beads per day. After an individual worker has completed 'a day's work', the foreman takes the full paddle to the first counter who declares the number of red beads they see. The second counter does the same. If the numbers announced are identical, the chief counter shouts out the number and the recorder notes the number of red beads on the large board.

The foreman conducts the process seriously, rejecting any comments from any of his fellow employees. After three days' work, the recorder counts up each worker's red bead count. The 3 red bead average target has been missed, predictably. The foreman then sacks the three worst performing workers. At the start of the fourth day, the foreman declares that if the remaining workers fail to hit the numerical target of three red beads per day, then the factory will be shut down. Furthermore, because the workforce has been cut by half, the three remaining workers are forced to carry out double shifts.

At the end of day four, the foreman expresses dismay at the failure of any of the workers to hit the company target of three red beads per worker per day. The company is closed. All 11 colleagues are declared jobless.

The lessons you can draw from the Red Bead Game are numerous. The workers are willing, but the system does not allow them to do a good job. All the workers are keen to do well. They follow the instructions precisely. Yet they know, even before the paddle enters the box of beads, that they cannot hit the numerical target set for them.

The foreman does not listen to any feedback. When I played the game with my GCSE business studies students, the first 'worker' suggested that he should be allowed to remove the red beads with his fingers and replace them with white beads. I rejected his suggestion in a dismissive manner, which silenced the rest of the workers. Even though the workers knew how to improve the system, there was no process for them to make their proposed improvements known.

Another learning point is that the foreman stipulates procedures that are irrelevant to the success of the task. Insisting that the workers use the paddle at a 47° angle is patent nonsense, yet the foreman insists upon that instruction every time a worker takes hold of the paddle. The counting of the red beads is assumed to be correct, even though it might be coincidence that the two counters declare identical results.

The measurement of the performance of the factory is purely numerical. The foreman is happy to make huge decisions about the number of employees and the future of the company, based solely upon basic data. The foreman does not question the data or check their reliability. The output is checked robotically by the three counters, without any check of the quality of the output.

Punishing the workers does not improve performance. Sacking three workers did nothing to reduce the prevalence of red beads. The remaining workers, fearful of being sacked too, were faced with the same production system and their fourth day output was, consequently, as poor as the three sacked workers' performances.

The person responsible for the system - and the only person with the authority to change the system - is the foreman, but instead of analysing the system, identifying its faults and remedying them, the foreman blames the willing workers, who were subsequently dismissed. Whilst the system was established, stable and precise, all that meant was that it produced poor outcomes consistently - 100% of the time.

So, when I reviewed the *Red Bead Game* with my business studies GCSE students, I asked them why they thought the company had failed. Danny replied, 'Well, Sir, they needed a Kaizen feedback system, didn't they?' And he was spot on. In companies that adopt the Kaizen philosophy, employees have two responsibilities: to perform their job as well as they can and to contribute to the continuous improvement of the companies' systems. If we translate that into a school context, we have to create conditions where classroom teachers accept the responsibility to teach as well as they can and to feed back to the school leadership on how to improve the school.

It is not hard to see how the *Red Bead Game* can highlight ineffective organisational practice:

- Systemic flaws prevent workers from producing high quality work;
- The leader of the organisation is deaf to feedback;
- Ineffective practice is made mandatory by a top-down model of management;
- Fear does not improve a worker's productivity;
- Data alone are not a measurement of quality, but are used in the decision-making process;
- Leaders blame the workers for organisational failure.

All too often, educators react badly to the suggestion that we can learn from the business world about how to run our organisations, but I have been a fan of Deming for as long as I can remember. His 'System of Profound Knowledge' is, essentially, an organisational model for continuous improvement – one where every single worker has a responsibility to help improve an organisation's systems. I have always said that I am not bothered about whether we adopt my idea; rather, it is the best ideas that I am seeking. These can come from anywhere in the organisation.

From his system, Deming derived his 14 Points and 7 Deadly Diseases, as well as the Deming Plan-Do-Study-Act (PDSA) cycle.

14 Points

1. Create constancy of purpose for improving products and services.
2. Adopt the new philosophy.
3. Cease dependence on inspection to achieve quality.
4. End the practice of awarding business on price alone; instead, minimise total cost by working with a single supplier.
5. Improve constantly and forever every process for planning, production and service.

6. Institute training on the job.
7. Adopt and institute leadership.
8. Drive out fear.
9. Break down barriers between staff areas.
10. Eliminate slogans, exhortations and targets for the workforce.
11. Eliminate numerical quotas for the workforce and numerical goals for management.
12. Remove barriers that rob people of pride of workmanship, and eliminate the annual rating or merit system.
13. Institute a vigorous programme of education and self-improvement for everyone.
14. Put everybody in the company to work accomplishing the transformation.

7 Deadly Diseases

1. Lack of constancy of purpose.
2. Emphasis on short-term profits.
3. Evaluation of performance, merit rating or annual review.
4. Mobility of management.
5. Management by use only of visible figures.
6. Excessive medical costs.
7. Excessive costs of liability.

Deming's 14 Points and 7 Deadly Diseases are easily applicable to education. Indeed, *The School for Quality Learning: Managing the School and Classroom the Deming Way* is the definitive guide to applying Deming's organisational model to schools (Crawford et al., 1993). But even if you do not read their book, modelling the relevant 14 Points and 7 Deadly Diseases would give you a school where:

- Every member of the school community knows the school's simple core purpose and set of values;
- Working to improve the quality of teaching is prioritised, rather than the observation of teaching;

- Continuous improvement is front and centre and the commitment to such a philosophy is school-wide;
- The CPD programme is expert, individually tailored and privileged;
- Leadership practices are developed throughout the organisation;
- Everyone works in a climate of mutual respect rather than fear;
- Structures promote colleagues working together on improving practice;
- Performance Management objectives are qualitative and the use of data-only objectives is banned;
- Teachers are guaranteed the pay rises coming to them;
- The sense that all staff are playing an important role in securing the success of the school is tangible;
- Qualifications are chosen to meet the needs of the students, not for accountability measures and performance league tables;
- School improvement is considered a long-term, incremental process.

And when it comes to school improvement, Deming's PDSA Cycle focuses upon ensuring that any aspect of the school's systems is continuously refined for improvement, rather than completely changed with no certainty of the new system being superior to what it replaced.

The PDSA Cycle is a systematic process for gaining valuable learning and knowledge for the continual improvement of any element of an organisation's systems. The cycle begins with the **Plan** step, which involves identifying a goal or purpose, formulating a theory, defining success metrics and putting a plan into action. These activities are followed by the **Do** step, in which the components of the plan are implemented, with the help of specific implementation activities. Next comes the **Study** step, where outcomes are monitored to test the validity of the plan for signs of progress and success or problems and areas for improvement. The Study step was important for Deming, because he considered studying and learning about the impact of your plan to be essential before you could truly understand how to make further incremental improvements. The **Act** step closes the cycle, integrating the learning generated by the entire process, which can be used to adjust the goal, change methods, reformulate a theory altogether, or broaden the learning-improvement cycle from a small-scale trial to a larger implementation plan. These four steps can be repeated over and over as part of a never-ending cycle of continual learning and improvement.

As Viviane Robinson says so brilliantly, we need to reduce change to increase improvement (Robinson, 2018). Change can be good or bad, but improvement makes an organisation better. Deming's work is concerned with removing all the barriers in an organisation, preventing willing workers from performing their job to the best of their ability.

In schools, we need to ensure that nothing prevents teachers from teaching well: a significant challenge. One way for school leaders to appreciate the obstacles facing teachers is to get back in the classroom and find out for themselves what it is like to teach in the school they lead. Robinson argues that when school leaders teach it enables them 'to learn in detail about the challenges facing teachers and the conditions they require to succeed [so that] any obstacles to creating those conditions for learning can be overcome'. Whether it is the fact that the new fancy screen the ICT department persuaded you to buy has no freeze function, so you cannot display slides and take the register simultaneously, or whether it is the lack of software for your visualiser, finding those things out first hand is invaluable for any school leader.

But even when I teach, I have no real idea of what it is like to be an NQT again, facing a class of 32 students along with all that entails. I have a dozen students, tops, in my office, with all the advantages that come with such a scenario. I need to know what I can do to help my colleagues do their job to the best of their ability, and it is only those colleagues who can tell me what that might be.

School leaders themselves actually teaching will not be enough for them to understand how their school works. They will need a systematic process for receiving feedback about the conditions facing the classroom teacher. At its most basic, a Feedback-to-Improve box in the staffroom that has easily accessible *pro formas* and pens, along with the option of remaining anonymous, will be a start. An electronic Feedback-to-Improve facility might be even better.

At Huntington, we have recently established a Workload Monitoring and Wellbeing Team comprising teaching and support staff. We have agreed that:

- We will establish an email feedback system, with the workload@ email address;
- We will also have an old-fashioned 'Suggestions Box' in the staffroom;
- The team will launch the feedback systems, not me;
- We will meet weekly. We have 15 members, so not everyone has to attend, but enough need to attend to make decisions, review feedback and respond appropriately and swiftly;
- We will undertake reviews of the big issues, like marking and feedback;
- We will use the feedback system to ask for solutions to problems that arise from the emails: for example, 'Does anyone have a good system for setting effective cover for years 7 & 8 lessons that is hassle-free for subject leaders and meaningful for students?'
- We will establish a 'You Said, We Did' board in the staffroom.

As headteacher, with an overview of the whole school's operations, I will attend every weekly meeting. Sometimes people will propose utterly obvious solutions to problems, but the solutions will have implications the proposers will not have appreciated, usually budget related. An extra period of Leadership and Management time a week, for instance, costs over £4,000 p.a. If the school budget has a projected surplus two years down the line of only £6,000, or 0.071% of the total budget, a proposal to give every subject leader one extra period of Leadership and Management time a week would cost over £100,000 p.a., which is an extra £500,000 five years down the line.

If we can create schools where the sense of hierarchy is reduced – something difficult in a country that is still, despite the new populism, saturated with a deference that is a legacy of the class system – so that any colleague can suggest improvement, then we can improve our schools relentlessly and continuously. Deming's philosophy gives school leaders the framework to achieve such a goal. One could argue that it will take courage from school leaders to institute a framework that downplays their importance; however, in schools, where leaders rely upon numerous other colleagues to perform as well as they can in order for those leaders to keep their jobs, I would argue that to have every single employee empowered to help improve the school is no courageous step – rather, it is plain common sense.

STAFF FIRST BLUEPRINT: SYSTEMATIC STAFF FEEDBACK

- The best idea is what we need, not your idea.
- School leaders in schools that put *staff first* gather as much intelligence about an issue as they can before making changes.
- In *blueprint schools*, leaders show wilful humility, encouraging feedback to ensure the school continues to improve.
- School leaders appreciate the obstacles facing teachers best by always being in classrooms, supporting staff and finding out for themselves what it is like to teach in the *blueprint school* they lead.
- *Blueprint school* leaders obsess about removing the obstacles that prevent teachers from doing their job successfully.

10. Succession planning

John Tomsett

As year 11 students tick off their completed GCSEs, the lessons in subjects for which they have finished their examinations are dedicated to revising for forthcoming examinations in other subjects. Those lessons can be hard to manage for the teachers. I stress to my colleagues, however, that, despite the challenges, I expect silent classrooms with purposeful revision.

So, a few years ago I was on tour of the school in mid-June when I heard music. I followed my ears and, the closer I got, the louder *Sister Sledge* became. I walked into a classroom to find that the year 11s – and their teacher – were, indeed, *lost in music*. It took several seconds for anyone to realise I had entered the room. When the teacher looked up, she was mortified. I raised my eyebrows, thanked the teacher and reminded the students that all of them would be sitting the second physics paper in less than 24 hours.

The subsequent email the teacher sent me was more than apologetic. It reeked of fear – fear of being damned forever by me for a harmless lapse on a hot afternoon with a year 11 class whose energy levels were waning. Her fear was very real. It would have been easy for me to damn that teacher forever; I didn't, but, for a moment on that hot summer afternoon, I was a bit irritated. The same teacher went on to secure a significant, well-deserved promotion to middle leadership and is about to spend half a term as an associate member of SLT.

School leaders only ever have a partial view of their organisation. The case of the disco-lesson teacher shows how easy it is to be negatively biased about a colleague's performance based upon a glimpse of their classroom practice. It is possible to have a positively biased view of a teacher in an equally misled way. Eradicating that bias is one of the many benefits of a highly effective succession planning process.

Despite the benefits of such a process, for literally years I have had 'succession planning' on my 'to do' list and have not done a single thing about it. As we struggle to find truly great staff, when we do, we need to develop and retain them (Rosenthal, J. et al. 2018). Effective succession planning is central to any healthy school. But succession planning is fraught with difficulties:

- Schools are busy, frenetic places, where the next set of results is the overriding priority for the vast majority of school leaders. The football manager syndrome, where you are only as good as your last set of results, often means that short-term goals trump long-term strategic planning;
- Succession planning can affect the whole school workforce: leaders can feel vulnerable and younger staff can feel unsettled if the process results in an inaccurate view of their aspirations and capabilities;
- Succession planning is often based on inaccurate, subjective data; when this happens, it creates suspicion, discontent and accusations of favouritism. It is important that the people in a school conducting succession planning processes are well trained;
- The lack of a clear process is another reason succession planning does more harm than good. Transparency is key when you are dealing with personnel issues, especially when it comes to succession planning. But securing that transparency, whilst ensuring that succession planning is a genuinely worthwhile activity, is a significant challenge;
- Ownership of the process is often unclear, and it is that kind of uncertainty that undermines any school's succession planning activities. Again, being utterly clear about who is doing what, when and why is vitally important if succession planning is going to do more good than harm;
- The other, quite school-specific issue around succession planning that schools must get right is rooted in the fact that teaching is

the core activity in a school; the development of teaching is the one thing above all else that school leaders must prioritise. So, system wide, we need thousands of classroom teachers doing a great job in the classroom, lesson after lesson, day after day, week after week, year in, year out. The thing is, in our profession teachers progress their careers through accepting leadership responsibilities and spending less time in the classroom as a result. Good teachers usually get promoted, when we need good teachers to keep on teaching!

- The previous bullet point gives rise to the last one: clarifying the difference between training teachers to be better teachers and developing their leadership attributes is crucial. Great teachers who get promoted might not necessarily prove to be great leaders, and we need to ensure that we differentiate between the two types of training.

The key is to shape a succession planning process that balances objective data evidence and the human sensitivities of discussing people's careers, a process that focuses upon putting *people first*. You also need an effective set of tools, which everyone understands, and well-trained colleagues to implement the process - colleagues who understand and can make the time commitment that sensitive succession planning demands.

Whilst there are challenges, there are numerous benefits of effective succession planning process that has a decent degree of objectivity and an even greater level of human investment woven into the process:

- If the human investment in the process is characterised by high quality conversations, you will find that you have greater leadership potential within your school than you could have ever predicted;
- Decisions around developing staff and promotions into leadership roles will be better because they will be so much more informed. A related benefit is that colleagues will feel that promotion decisions are fair and accurate;
- If you can deliver genuine career development opportunities, the experience will help create a happier, healthier, more motivated school staff and improve retention rates;

- In a school that puts *staff first*, effective succession planning practices will create a deeper commitment to the ethos of your school because the ethical humanity of your processes will be appreciated by colleagues;
- If you get succession planning right, it is likely that improved retention rates create year-on-year marginal gains in the quality of the education enjoyed by students, as greater knowledge of the school's systems and cultural norms deepens staff expertise.

When we finally designed a succession planning process at Huntington School, we wanted it to achieve three things:

1. To provide us with a summary overview of our staffing from which we could identify colleagues we were in danger of losing and identify posts for which we had no immediate successor, so that we would retain key colleagues and grow future leaders;
2. To provide our existing colleagues with a personalised CPD offer that goes beyond the training we provide to support our more general school development priorities;
3. To recruit new staff, attracted by our proactive approach to career development.

Our first move was to research industry practices. We explored a number of 9-box models used in businesses. A 9-box model is a widely used performance and potential matrix that is an incredibly helpful tool for succession planning and development. Our model is composed of 9 boxes arranged on an x- and y-axis grid, with potential measured along the x-axis, and performance along the y-axis. Other models flip the axes. We chose to have performance on the y-axis in our 9-box model to ensure that the expert classroom teacher was in the top left-hand box, emphasising the importance of teaching as the principal activity in our profession. The top right-hand box is composed of those ranking high in both performance and leadership capacity. Conversely, the bottom left-hand box is the place for those ranking low in both measures.

The model is a catalyst for constructive dialogue and, in turn, will facilitate a conversation with individual colleagues. The idea behind the matrix is that by identifying how each colleague fits into the grid, you can better understand each colleague's current thinking about their performance and aspirations, and then how they might be developed and retained.

For all 9-box models, you need to design a leadership competency model. Such models are made to highlight the leadership skills and behaviours that contribute to peak performance. Now, it is easy to recognise the past performance of individuals, but identifying their potential is a complicated task. A common difficulty experienced by users of the 9-box model is to accurately position their candidates on the matrix, as well as determining a strategy for their retention or succession plan.

Our work with Network Rail helped. Its leadership competency model has three broad competencies: 'Sociability'; 'Thinking'; 'Aspiration'. It includes the competency 'Resilience' within 'Aspiration'. We thought that 'Resilience' deserved a separate area of its own for several reasons: as a teacher, teaching for five hours a day requires physical and mental resilience; as a school leader, coping with the level of responsibility that comes with the job requires significant levels of resilience; and, finally, just to get up on a dark Monday morning in late November and get to work, we all need to be resilient!

And it is hard to be a truly great teacher and a highly effective school leader without having expert 'Knowledge'. Consequently, the five competencies in our leadership competency model are: 'Sociability'; 'Thinking'; 'Aspiration'; 'Resilience'; 'Knowledge'. Our leadership competency model is called the STARK model (it was the 'STAR' model until we added 'Knowledge'; in some ways it is good because, before we added 'Knowledge', it could have been known as the 'RATS' model).

Each 'STARK' competency has three descriptors:

STARK Self Reflection Tool

Attribute		Descriptor	Example
Sociability	Empathy:	appreciate others' points of view and understand others' motivations.	
	Influence:	has the capacity to influence different people using a range of interpersonal styles.	
	Respect, honesty, kindness:	demonstrates consistently professional conduct which exemplifies our values.	
Thinking	Problem analysis:	identifies issues and problems early, adopting a rigorous, analytical diagnostic approach.	
	Creative thinking:	generates new and different perspectives within which to understand situations	
	Judgement:	balances reflection with action to reach sound and practical decisions	
Aspiration	Drive:	determined to make a broad impact on our school, which is aligned with our core values and is rooted in a desire to make a positive difference to our students' lives.	
	Commitment:	to developing their career path whilst maintaining a certain wilful humility.	
	Proactive:	takes the initiative to make things happen; puts ambitious ideas into practice and follows through to completion.	
Resilience	Tenacity:	persistence in seeing things through despite sometimes difficult challenges.	
	Grit:	recovers from setbacks.	
	Self-awareness:	possesses a clear, unvarnished understanding of their strengths and weaknesses and uses this to manage their behaviour and judge situations effectively.	
Knowledge	Subject Knowledge:	expert level of subject knowledge and pedagogy	
	General educational knowledge:	good level of awareness of current local, regional and national educational issues.	
	Continuous Learner:	actively seeks out opportunities to update and increase knowledge	

The 9-box model we consequently went on to develop is illustrated below:

Huntington '9-Box' model

The final element of the succession planning process was to shape a menu of development opportunities. We could not be exhaustive when drafting the menu of development opportunities and nor did we want to be; if, in our succession planning conversations, we show colleagues the menu, they will stop thinking and choose an opportunity from the menu. The key thing was to ask individuals what ideas they might have about meeting their own development needs. If they draw a blank, then we can produce the menu for discussion.

Career Stage	STARK Qualities	Development Opportunities	Linked Reading Resources
NQT/RQT	Sociability	Share experiences with fellow NQTs/RQTs in the NQT/RQT meetings Attend 'How to be an Effective Coach' training	Resources can be found: P drive>Central admin>Resources> STARK and Staff Development Programme>NQT/RQT
	Thinking	Work alongside a more experienced colleague on their Inquiry Question to develop an aspect of your pedagogy through a short research project	• Bill Rogers by Tom Sherrington • Relationships at School by Tom Sherrington
	Aspiration	Access subject groups/networks Contribute to the Research School newsletter by writing/co-writing a blog with the RS team Attend workshop on applications/interviews	• Strategies for deescalating behaviour • 10 Top Tips for Parents' Evenings • Parent Evening Infographic • Parents' Evenings
	Resilience	Meet fortnightly with mentor Attend HS resilience session	• 10 Ways to Differentiate in the Classroom • Differentiation and Inclusion

	Knowledge	Arrange to observe an 'expert teacher' within your dept
		RQT peer-mentoring of an NQT
		Attend session 'An introduction to Research School'
		Attend a Research School twilight
		Attend JMT session on social media profile and presence
		Attend MJ session on how to write a blog/article
			in the Classroom
			• Top Tips for an Inclusive Classroom
			• Effective Questioning & Talk
			• Great Teaching Great Questioning
			  Tom Sherrington
			• Guide to Questioning
			  in the Classroom

Expert Teacher	Sociability	Be a mentor to colleagues who need to improve Attend 'How to be an Effective Coach' training	Resources can be found: P drive>Central admin>Resources> STARK and Staff Development Programme>Expert Teacher
	Thinking	Share expertise in the SDP Sessions	
	Aspiration	Facilitate external CPD opportunities, e.g. visit other schools Contribute to the Research School newsletter by writing a blog/article on area of expertise	
	Resilience	Share expertise in establishing and maintaining a balance between work/life Attend HS resilience session	
	Knowledge	Observe other colleagues Attend subject-specific CPD Attend session 'An introduction to Research School' Attend a Research School twilight on a subject of interest (secondary literacy, SEND, HW) Share expertise in a dept TLF Attend JMT session on social media profile and presence Attend MJ session on how to write a blog/article	

Future Middle Leader	Sociability	Influence – lead a dept TLF Coach/mentor within dept Attend 'How to be an Effective Coach' training	Resources can be found: P drive>Central admin>Resources> STARK and Staff Development Programme>Future Middle Leader • Delivering Excellence. The role of Middle Leaders • SecEd Guide to Middle Leadership • Change – Little Book of Managing Change • Switch by Chip and Dan Heath • The Changing Face of Middle Leadership • Incomplete Leader • Strategies for being more assertive • Compelling Leadership – Paul Browning • Middle Leadership Schools Week article
	Thinking	Diagnose/identify an issue in the dept and lead on a solution Attend Research School Curriculum course Become a member of the Junior Leadership Team	
	Aspiration	Attend CDG Lead on a strand of subject development priorities Attend workshop on applications/interviews Attend Andy Buck Leadership session	
	Resilience	Access a coaching experience Attend training on conflict resolution Attend HS resilience session	
	Knowledge	Attend external CPD/external subject leads meeting & lead in dept Shadow an ML Attend session 'An introduction to Research School' Attend JMT session on social media profile and presence	
Future Senior Leader	Sociability	Influence – contribute to/lead whole school training Act as a coach for a fellow ML Lead part of a PD meeting/cycle Attend 'How to be an Effective Coach' training	Resources can be found: P drive>Central admin>Resources> STARK and Staff Development> Future Senior Leader • HBR The one type of leader who can turn around a failing school • Viviane Robinson on school leadership • Switch by Chip and Dan Heath • Incomplete Leader • Compelling Leadership- Paul Browning • Butterflies for School Improvement • ARK Lessons Learned • Characteristics of successful MATs • 7 strong claims about school leadership • Curriculum led budget planning • School Leadership Review DfE
	Thinking	Identify a whole school problem & lead on a solution	
	Aspiration	Become an Associate member of SLT Lead a WSTLF Shadow a member of Research School Represent the school at an external event/meeting Present to governors Attend workshop on applications/interviews Attend Andy Buck Leadership session Attend Steve Munby presentation on leadership	
	Resilience	Attend HS resilience session	
	Knowledge	Observe a colleague out of the dept who is an expert Join Twitter/write a blog Contribute to the planning and delivery of a Research School twilight (secondary literacy, SEND, HW) Attend Day 1 of the Research School Pupil Premium course 29/01 Attend JMT session on social media profile and presence	

Future Pastoral Leader	Sociability	Contribute to a Pastoral WSTLF
		Attend 'How to be an Effective Coach' training
			Resources can be found:
			P drive>Central admin>Resources>
			STARK and Staff Development>
			Future Pastoral Leader
			• National College Managing
			  Behaviour Think Piece
			• DfE Mental Health and Behaviour in
			  Schools. A guide
			• Resilience – how to build it
			• Young Minds. The
			  Resilient Classroom
			• Developing Behaviour Management
			  for ITT
			• IPPR Education, education...
			  Mental Health
			• DfE Counselling in Schools. A
			  blueprint for the future
			• Strategies for being more assertive
			• Switch by Chip and Dan Heath
			• A Pastoral Leadership Guide.
			  Marilyn Nathan

	Thinking	Work closely with a student who relies on pastoral support – case study	
	Aspiration	Attend & contribute to an HDC Shadow a pastoral leader Attend workshop on applications/interviews Attend Andy Buck Leadership session	
	Resilience	Access a coaching experience Attend training on conflict resolution Attend HS resilience session	
	Knowledge	Attend external CPD/external subject leads meeting Attend Day 1 of the Research School Pupil Premium course 29/01 Shadow a member of the pastoral/SEND team Attend JMT session on social media profile and presence	

This menu only works if you have planned who is responsible for ensuring that the development opportunities are realised. The worst thing that could happen is for the teacher to be offered the development opportunity but then no one takes responsibility for following through on that promise. When it comes to succession planning and individualised professional development, better to promise nothing at all than to make false promises.

Once we had a process to test out, we approached a small number of teacher colleagues at different stages of their careers to pilot what we had shaped up. They helped the development team eliminate many of the potential aspects of our process that might cause upset to colleagues. Governors were fully on board, realising that the proactive development of staff is crucial to sustaining a thriving school.

We then presented the process to the whole teaching, teaching assistant and cover team. The colleagues who were in the pilot played a major role in the introductory presentation, which helped enormously in convincing colleagues that the new succession planning process was a genuinely supportive, unthreatening initiative that aimed to help the institution whilst providing colleagues with personalised professional development.

At the end of the introductory presentation, colleagues were asked to complete the STARK competency grid with an example of when they have shown each of the 15 descriptors. The guidance was clear: complete the grid instinctively. If it takes you a significant length of time to think of an example, then leave the descriptor blank. The blanks are important for the next stage: the succession planning conversation.

The process at Huntington was kept as simple as possible. Crucially, it involved significant human investment. The whole system will only work if colleagues believe that those leading the process are genuinely interested in investing time and effort in helping them develop.

Each teacher, teaching assistant and cover supervisor had a 30-minute conversation with their Performance Development Reviewer (PDR). Those who developed the process trained the PDR team, using scripts based on the Whitmore GROW (Goal, Reality, Options, Will) model of coaching and a video-recorded modelled conversation.

The outcome of each conversation saw the member of staff plot themselves on the 9-box model, identify their possible development opportunities and discuss their career aspirations. The data from these conversations were kept on the simplest spreadsheet. Administration was kept to a minimum; conversations were the important thing.

As an SLT, we wanted to feel confident about any analysis of the data for future planning. Consequently, once we had finished the full round of conversations, as an SLT we reviewed the 9-box outcomes. We wanted to see what consistency we had. If X colleague and Y colleague both independently plotted themselves on the 9-box model as 'Good' at the end of their STARK conversation, does that make sense to us? What further intelligence about those individuals emerged from the conversations?

The conversations took place for real between November and January, and the development opportunities were delivered between February and July. At the Performance Development reviews in September and October, they were evaluated, and the process began again in November. Nothing is rushed. Everything is planned in detail and evaluated intelligently.

One of the most useful outcomes of the succession planning process is the overview it gives you of staffing at whole school level, department level and individual level. Here is an example of what a departmental level analysis might look like and the new intelligence such analysis can provide:

Worked example: the Latin Department

In the case of the Latin department above, it is easy to identify the three key actions that arise from the succession planning analysis:

1. There is no immediate successor for the subject leader, so how do we develop the assistant subject leader (ASL in the graphic) to be able to step up into that post should it become vacant?
2. Not everyone is an expert teacher, so another focus is to improve the quality of teaching within the Latin department.
3. The Strong Performers and the Rising colleagues need to be offered development opportunities that will help retain them and prepare them for future leadership roles within the school.

Such analysis can crystallise formally what a school leader might feel intuitively but has had neither the time nor the tools to address explicitly. This example highlights why, institutionally, putting *staff first* by investing in succession planning can ensure, in a very deliberate sense, that our students are taught by the very best teachers.

Beyond departmental analysis, our model gives you a central record of the whole staff's CPD needs, from which your school-based CPD team can plan personalised development opportunities for each individual colleague.

If a succession planning process is going to have a chance of being successful, all those involved in the process have to believe that there is something in it for them. And you have to cultivate transparency and trust in the process, something that is difficult if your school does not, genuinely, put *staff first*.

Beyond the sensitivities inherent in succession planning, those leading the process need to accept accountability and responsibility for the quality of the process and the outcomes. Those leaders must have the clarity of vision to plan for the school's future staffing and leadership needs, not solely the institution's current needs. And they must have the discipline to largely ignore immediate concerns, instead pursuing the longer-term outcomes of effective school staff succession planning. It is also important, when considering future staffing structures, to think about the roles you need for your school to be an effective school before you think about individual members of staff.

It is crucial that school leaders remain particularly aware of the potential negative impact of a succession planning process that does not consider the very human aspects of discussing colleagues' performance and their future aspirations.

At Huntington, we adopted certain practices to ensure that our succession planning process avoided some of the pitfalls facing any school trying to plan for the future whilst coping with the present.

We ensured that the leadership team that was going to engage with colleagues was fully involved in shaping the succession planning process. This meant that any vulnerabilities the leadership team felt about developing those who might succeed it were reflected upon way before the STARK conversations took place.

The development opportunities were authentic. We had to ensure they were realised. And we asked two key questions about the colleagues we were supporting. Not just are they ready for a new leadership role, but, if they are not, then how do we get them ready? The development opportunities fell into three categories: experience, exposure and education. Some, like leading whole school CPD, were an authentic *experience* that involved taking on leadership responsibility; some, like being a shadow member of the SLT for half a term, were an *exposure* to a role that would help individuals decide whether or not it was for them; and there were *educative* opportunities, like attending an external CPD course.

We emphasised the benefits to the organisation and to individuals, and gave leaders responsibility for growing others. Indeed, as Michael Fullan claims, 'to a certain extent, a school leader's effectiveness in creating a culture of sustained change will be determined by the leaders he or she leaves behind' (Fullan, 2002).

One of the things I did as headteacher was to be open about the longer vision of the school. Huntington School will operate way beyond each one of us. When you are in the thick of it, dealing successfully with myriad challenges day in, day out, it is easy to feel indispensable, to think that the school could not possibly operate without your leadership - all of which is, of course, nonsense. Within a week of my retirement, staff at Huntington will not be able to recall whether I was called John or Tom...

We must all have a plan for what we do beyond our current role. We can have several new stages of our lives and careers, and having a plan for the future makes the present feel more precious and less demanding.

We must show a broader view of our role as leaders in the education system, not just in our own schools. One of the unforeseen consequences of effective succession planning that provides genuine development opportunities is the loss of promising staff who leave you precisely because you developed them. That is a good thing. You are helping make the system stronger. In your school, new vacancies give aspirant staff fresh opportunities. Young blood will be attracted to your school precisely because you develop people and enable them to progress in their careers. Effective succession planning is a win-win strategy.

We have lots of people working in schools, but too often there is a marked division between teachers and support staff - in the worst schools, they are designated as *non-teaching staff*, defined by what they don't do.

It's important to do all we can to create the sense of a single staff. Where possible, all policies and practices should apply consistently to teachers and support staff alike.

Teachers must remember two things about our support staff.

Firstly, that they earn a great deal less than teachers. The *Whitehall Study* in 1967 concluded that '[m]en in the lowest grade (messengers, doorkeepers, etc.) had a mortality rate three times higher than that of men in the highest grade (administrators) and that more attention should be paid to the social environ-ments, job design, and the consequences of income inequality' (Whitehall I, 1967). Colleagues who have no autonomy over what they do are the ones who can feel most stressed, whilst headteachers can make choices about nearly every aspect of their working lives.

Secondly, without support staff, teachers would be stuffed!

So, the next phase of our succession planning development will focus upon our support staff. Our thoughts are that a succession planning programme for support staff would be slightly different from our STARK system. All teachers do largely the same thing. Promotion for teachers is about taking on leadership responsibilities, but they still teach and their increased responsibility is about the leadership of teaching and learning; *remember that TLR stands for 'Teaching and Learning Responsibility'.* If you are the school's examinations officer, how-ever, where next for you? It might be a case of discussing transferable skills and giving support staff colleagues the chance to broaden their experience with a taste of an entirely different role.

And the examinations officer is a critical role; if the examinations officer wins the lottery and flees to Barbados (we prefer that than the alternative of going under a bus), the school would be in some trouble if it has not developed a potential successor. Risk number two in our Risk Management Assessment for the Governors' Staffing committee is: 'There is a risk that we fail to meet deadline for payroll which could be the result of having no systematic back-up cover for our Finance Manager that may lead to staff not being paid, a fall in morale, a dent to our reputation as an employer and an inability to recruit good staff.' Have we got all the critical support functions of school covered with back-up staffing? All this is vital if a school is going to function effectively. Succession planning for critical roles in the support staff structure is equally important in many ways to succession planning for teachers. When we put *staff first*, it means *all* staff, not just teachers.

Ultimately, at the heart of highly effective succession planning are two key factors: an unyielding focus upon the human aspect of the process and a school's wilful determination to see the process through. How well a school can attend to these two factors will have a significant impact on its ability to effectively find and develop its next generation of leaders.

Finally, if your succession planning process is transparent and operates in a culture of trust where leaders genuinely put *staff first*, even the greatest *Sister Sledge* fans will be able to prosper in their careers.

STAFF FIRST BLUEPRINT: SUCCESSION PLANNING

- *Blueprint school* leaders have to be extensively trained in how to develop people and how to gain a systematic overview of succession planning.
- Succession planning in *blueprint schools* is explicitly woven into the school's systems.
- The individual career development needs of colleagues are prioritised in *blueprint schools* that put *staff first*.
- Senior leaders invest significant amounts of their time in supporting colleagues with their professional development.
- *Blueprint school* leaders know that, even if they lose colleagues to other schools because they have been trained and developed well, their reputation for investing in staff will ensure they will be able to recruit good staff in turn.

11. Developing a *staff-first* culture across a school-led system

Jonny Uttley

Much has changed in English schools over the last ten years. Some of that change has been for the better, some for the worse, and much of that change is still subject to fierce debate. Many of the terms we discuss today were unheard of ten years ago: the English Baccalaureate (Ebacc), Progress 8, systematic synthetic phonics, multi-academy trusts, off-rolling, gaming. Twitter has connected teachers and leaders and enabled collaboration, sharing practice and debate; it has also facilitated unhelpful binary arguments that do little to improve schools and reflect badly on the profession. Perhaps the most worrying development of all is the notion of 'toxic schools' - places where teachers feel fearful and undervalued, where the notion of professional trust has evaporated, and where leaders make decisions in the best interests of the school as an institution rather than the people in the school.

There are a multitude of theories for the origin of toxic schools. Some blame Ofsted or league tables; others look to the growth of multi-academy trusts or the DfE's various policy attempts to speed up the process of academisation; still others point fingers at individual school or trust leaders and call into question their personal motivations for leading. It is unhelpful that explanations for the causes of toxicity, at times, seem to be proxies for broader political views. For example, while having reservations about academisation because of the removal of local control is a legitimate and often sincerely held view, blaming all academies and trusts is an inaccurate over-simplification and ignores the fact that there is both exemplary leadership in many academies and still some poor practice in some maintained schools.

In Chapter 8, we argued that Ofsted has had an inordinate impact on the way schools operate, and there is little doubt that it has. The fear of the disastrous consequences of a poor inspection judgement has been a powerful driver of many schools' behaviour, and is based on too many good school leaders being on the sharp end of negative experiences of inspection. But the fundamental cause of toxicity goes deeper than this. Since 2010, we, as leaders, have all been stuck in one big zero sum game in which too many leaders have given in to the perverse incentives the system has created.

Tom Sherrington has written extensively on this, most notably in 2015 in 'Nicky Morgan v The Bell Curve' (Sherrington, 2015) and again a year later in 'Rethinking Success in the Post-Gaming Zero Sum Era' (Sherrington, 2016). Since then, the work of FFT Education Datalab has repeatedly shone a light on the limitations of Progress 8 as a true measure of school performance and the shortcomings of the comparable outcomes approach to key stage 2 tests. Dave Thomson's piece 'Progress 8 scores for most schools aren't that different' in February 2019 was particularly powerful (Thomson, 2019a).

Put into very simple terms, grades at key stages 4 and 5 are awarded using comparable outcomes: 'This means that, under usual circumstances, the aim is that "roughly the same proportion of students will achieve each grade as in the previous year"' (Benton, 2016, internal quotation marks indicating Benton's use of another source, Ofqual, 2012). At key stage 2, the expected standard is fixed at 100 and the performance of all students nationally is then distributed comparatively between 80 and 120. This means that GCSE, A level or key stage 2 performance can never show whether young people and schools are actually getting better. When we then add in Progress 8 and key stage 2 progress measures that simply compare schools with each other, we have created a system where for one school to show it has got 'better', another school has to be shown to have got 'worse'.

And so a model of school leadership has developed that puts winning the zero sum game ahead of all else. One school, part of a well-known multi-academy trust, states on its website as part of its vision, '[we] will see the academy ranked in the top 1% of secondary schools by 2020'. If that is the be-all and end-all of a school's ambition, then it is natural to seek advantage over other schools to ensure that your school comes out on top. At key stage

2, it made sense to narrow the curriculum and hothouse children for Standard Assessment Tests (SATs); at secondary school, it became a rational school performance strategy to identify 'anchor' students and look to move them to a school roll elsewhere to prevent them appearing on the school's results; if the ultimate ambition is to be in the top 1%, then why encourage students to enter 'hard' qualifications like languages when BTEC Sport or BTEC Health and Social Care are nearly 2.5 points 'easier'? (Thomson, 2019b)

Schools that have put performance measures above all else have also often developed systems and processes that undermine staff confidence, development and wellbeing. Every day, many teachers across the country go to work in schools where monitoring and evaluation systems are set up to find fault and catch people out; they are subject to processes that fail any test of common sense, like the senior leader with a degree in chemistry feeding back to the Spanish graduate on where they identified a slowing of progress in a set of year 11 exercise books in which they did not understand a single word the students had written! Too many teachers are still told exactly how to teach each lesson, but are held to account if results don't go according to plan. Schools across the country still make staff jump through hoops to get a £2,000 pay rise they are frankly entitled to and call it 'performance-related pay'. Professional trust has been replaced by a culture of audit and compliance, something Andrew Schleicher of the OECD argues is driving innovation from the profession and holding back standards (Gibbons, 2018).

Our blueprint is not just for individual schools or trusts; it is a blueprint for the system. At its heart is the very simple proposition that school leaders should do the right thing, and the more school leaders who choose to do the right thing, the better the system becomes.

In the last few years, the notion of 'ethical leadership' has once again come to the fore. To a large degree, this has been a response to growing concerns about the toxicity of the system. Leaders who have quietly gone about doing the right thing have begun to seek a common language to articulate what we do and to demonstrate its power. The Association of School and College Leaders (ASCL), the National Governors Association, the Chartered College of Teaching and others have identified the promotion of an ethical framework for school leadership as one of the most pressing and significant issues for the

Ethical Leadership Qualities
Competencies and Behaviours

Competency	We do this by	Behaviours
Trust – leaders are trustworthy and reliable	• Earning trust by being reliable, consistent, credible, honest, humble, courageous and kind. • Prioritising our long-term purpose first, above short-term goals. • Managing emotions and helping others to manage their emotions. • Keeping promises. • Having a genuine interest in others, seeking to understand the whole person. • Using a range of communication skills in a range of circumstances with a range of people, developing rapport, trust and a deeper level of understanding.	• Live our values every day. • Take every opportunity to communicate and apply our values, showing how they guide and inform decisions. • Do what is right, rather than what is popular. • Be accountable to your colleagues, students and the community, acting in service to others. • Influence the behaviour of those around you. • Take time to develop high trust relationships. • Act selflessly to protect and enable the trust to achieve its purpose.
Wisdom – leaders use experience, knowledge and insight	• Developing knowledge and expertise, then sharing knowledge to enable collaborative convergence. • Seeking learning opportunities, learning from mistakes and failures, and sharing the learning with others. • Having, and encouraging in others, a growth mindset. Believing in the potential of others and creating a safe learning environment, with systems that enable sharing of knowledge, collaboration and innovation. • Recruiting knowledgeable, skilled experts and learning from them, helping them to flourish productively.	• Share knowledge and expertise with others, developing a learning culture where people are encouraged to research, share and develop ideas collaboratively. • Anticipate the future and help people prepare for change. • Be open to opportunities and commit to learning every day. • Recruit people who may be more expert than you, learn from them and develop next generation ethical leaders.
Kindness – leaders demonstrate respect, generosity of spirit, understanding and good temper	• Demonstrating respect, generosity of spirit, understanding and good temper. • Being kind to others, seeking opportunities to serve others for the greater good. • Leading with compassion and care, listening and engaging with the person, not the job role. • Using high levels of emotional intelligence, developing a sense of belonging and contribution. Building trust and rapport with others, by acknowledging, empowering and elevating others.	• Be humble. • Bring your authentic self to work. • Have the courage to be genuine. • Lead with compassion, empathy and kindness. • Show people you care about them. • Search out opportunities for acts of kindness, a selfless act intended to bring help, happiness or joy to another person.
Justice – leaders are fair and work for the good of all children	• Doing what is right, rather than what is popular or easy. • Ensuring we live and breathe our sense of purpose and values in the way we behave, interact with others, make decisions and communicate. • Ensuring rules are necessary and applying them in a consistent, transparent and fair way, whilst allowing for discretion and common sense. • Valuing difference, building diverse teams and encouraging others to behave responsibly towards the community and the environment. • Seeing and acknowledging other people's strengths, knowledge and skills. Encouraging people to share and build on their strengths and successes across and beyond the trust.	• Be accountable to others and serve our purpose. • Be morally brave and stand up and be counted for what you believe in. • Do the right thing, which might not be the easiest or most popular option.
Service – leaders are conscientious and dutiful	• Behaving in a dutiful, conscientious way, demonstrating humility and self-control to build great schools. • Removing barriers and blockers to enable others to achieve their goals, for the benefit of young people, maximising strengths and helping others to see possibilities and seize opportunities. • Viewing systems, methods, models and techniques as a means to an end, removing or changing them if they prove to be ineffective. • Leaving our egos at the door and putting ourselves in the service of others. Standing aside and championing others and their ideas and contributions.	• Walk the talk and behave in an honest, open and fair way. • Channel ambition into our schools, not ourselves, developing successors. • Have intense professional will and personal humility. • Have a systematic approach to manage the execution and delegation of tasks and be reliable. • Create new habits through the accumulation of different choices.
Courage – leaders work courageously in the best interests of children and young people	• Striving for honesty, sharing the full story wherever possible and as early as possible. • Looking in the mirror when something goes wrong. • Sacrificing personal or short-term goals for the achievement of longer-term, sustainable, shared goals. • Relishing challenge and finding strength in each other, building organisational resilience. • Remaining calm, optimistic and positive in the face of adversity, adapting to changing circumstances and helping others to move forward.	• Give the whole truth, the back-story and the why. • Have skilfully led difficult conversations. • Aim to exceed expectations and achieve things you thought you couldn't.
Optimism – leaders are positive and encouraging	• Believing in our own ability, and the ability of others, to do what is right to change the world for the better. • Remaining positive and encouraging, despite sometimes experiencing setbacks, challenges and pressures. Helping others to maximise opportunities, overcome challenges and celebrate success. • Being respectful, kind and sensitive to others and responding well to ambiguity, making positive use of the opportunities it presents.	• Believe the best in others, help people progress and unlock their potential. • Remain calm, professional, reliable and consistent. • Manage your emotions well and help others do the same. • Have and encourage a growth mindset, believing abilities and talents can be cultivated. • Set yourself challenging goals and work hard to achieve them.
Vision	• Anticipating the future and helping people ready themselves for change. Thinking strategically, researching, gathering, analysing and assessing information, seeking opportunities for organisational development. • Believing in the potential of others; helping them be the best they can be. • Quickly taking in new information and translating that into recommendations, decisions, plans and projects. • Translating complex data and information into understandable messages for a variety of audiences. Sharing compelling stories that others can understand, believe in and work towards.	• Scan the horizon, read and research, share learning with others and collaborate to consider options, obstacles and risks. • Think creatively, formulate strategies, plans and projects, aligned to our vision and values. • Actively share a compelling vision, encourage people to get involved, maximise their strengths, develop colleagues and see opportunities to elevate them. • Translate complex information with the intended audience in mind and communicate positively.

system (ASCL, 2019). I regularly speak about ethical leadership at events and I am always greeted with smiles, nods and general agreement that this is a good thing.

And herein lies the difficulty. I have never met anyone who describes themselves as an unethical school leader, and yet we all recognise unethical behaviour. Whenever I stand in front of year 7 students in a hall on the first day in September, I say that they may not know all the school rules yet, but they all know the difference between good behaviour and bad behaviour. Similarly, in school leadership, we all know that some things are wrong, no matter what.

For example, it must always be wrong to encourage a family to 'educate' their child at home rather than recording an exclusion; it must always be wrong to register a student somewhere else to improve a league table position; it must always be wrong to enter first language English speakers for a second language English qualification. And while not everything is utterly clear-cut in a world of comparable outcomes, it is difficult to defend leadership behaviour that undermines other school leaders who are desperately trying to do the right thing.

At the Education Alliance, ethical leadership underpins everything we do; it is about doing what we know is right: trusting our colleagues professionally; being kind and brave; behaving in ways that specifically reduce fear and anxiety in our schools; and reminding ourselves always that we are here to serve others. We have rewritten our leadership standards around an ethical framework and clearly articulate the behaviours leaders must show. We recruit around these standards, and leadership development is about supporting leaders to get even better. This isn't some soft and woolly nice-to-have; we have set very high standards for ourselves that are not always easy to live up to.

We have to remember that all the micro interactions we have as school leaders with colleagues will, incrementally, define the culture of our schools. From our trust board down, we believe living by these publicly declared standards is the most important facet of creating schools that great teachers want to work in and stay in.

The critical importance of ethical leadership, however, goes far beyond the behaviour and decision-making of individual school leaders and leadership teams. It has to underpin the entirety of a school or trust's operations; what it seeks to achieve; how it measures itself; and, in the case of a trust, how it grows. Because although little in education is ever truly black and white, two distinct approaches have emerged. In one approach, the focus is on results above performance; rapid growth; systems that ensure compliance; and a culture of high anxiety and low trust with high accountability but low autonomy. It is one of the great shames of recent years that this model has been courted, lauded, and held up to be copied, and that the myth that any school can be 'transformed' in two terms has perpetuated. Meanwhile, leaders and teachers are leaving the profession in record numbers.

There is, however, another way. There are lots of great leaders in academies, maintained schools and trusts who lead differently. The focus is on performance before results; growth is deliberate and not for its own sake; systems are about improvement, not compliance; the culture is of low anxiety and high trust; accountability is high but levels of autonomy are high too. Leaders in these schools are driven by a strong sense of moral purpose and have the wisdom to understand the central importance of vibrant work cultures in retaining teachers in the profession. They also have the courage to lead in this way and to care about young people and staff in other leaders' schools, despite the fact that the accountability system - particularly the comparable nature of league tables - makes it excruciatingly difficult at times.

High performing schools and trusts	• Rapid growth • Results driven • Low autonomy; high accountability • Low professional trust • Systems driven by policy compliance • High challenge; high threat • Weak sense of moral purpose • Negative work environment • Unsustainable • Toxic for broader system	• Deliberate growth • Performance driven • High autonomy; high accountability • High professional trust • Systems driven by performance and improvement • High challenge; low threat • Strong sense of moral purpose • Vibrant work environment • Sustainable • Deep commitment to broader system
Low performing schools and trusts	• Inconsistent growth • Results driven • Low autonomy; inconsistent accountability • Low professional trust • Systems driven by external accountability • Inconsistent challenge; high threat • Weak sense of moral purpose • Negative work environment • Unsustainable • Low performance creates problems for broader system	• Lacks growth • Personality driven • High autonomy; low accountability • Laissez-faire approach to trust • Weak and inconsistent systems • Low challenge; low threat • Confused sense of moral purpose • Pleasant work environment • Unsustainable • Low performance creates problems for broader system

At the Education Alliance, we have had honest and open discourse at trust board level about how different schools and trusts operate and what we want to be. Alongside our ethical leadership qualities, we have created our trust development framework. Trustees are clear that our schools must seek to operate in the top right-hand box (see graphic on previous page) at all times. A *blueprint school* that puts *staff first* will operate here too.

When Ofsted inspected Driffield School, our sponsored academy previously in Special Measures, Scott, the headteacher, was very clear with the inspection team about the framework within which he operates and the focus he places on putting *staff first*. Scott described the trust as putting an 'ethical umbrella' over the school. In the final feedback, the lead inspector praised the ethical decisions the school had made around alternative provision, alternatives to exclusions and the genuine focus upon staff wellbeing, describing the school's 30-month turnaround as 'rapid' and, crucially, 'sustainable'.

When John became headteacher of Huntington School in 2007, I was a head of year there. That September 2007 training day was the first time I had heard a headteacher discuss the school's GCSE results from the summer without comparing them with those of other schools. He said we should never take pleasure in 'beating' another school, as that means we are pleased young people in that other school hadn't done as well as our young people, which was morally indefensible for an educator. A leader in a *blueprint school* will think beyond what is in the interests of their own school as an institution and will think about the impact of all their decisions on the school down the road. By doing so, it makes it easier for the leader down the road to put their *staff first* too. The more people who lead this way, the better the system will become, because it is through our collective behaviour that the system will thrive or fail.

STAFF FIRST BLUEPRINT: STAFF FIRST CULTURE

- Our current accountability system has created a zero sum game; despite that, *blueprint school* leaders don't worry about 'winning'; they have a commitment to improve the whole school system.
- The ethical behaviour of *blueprint school* leadership creates a safe yet challenging culture in schools and attracts people to the profession.

- Rather than talking generally about 'ethical leadership', *blueprint schools* clearly articulate the leadership behaviours they expect and live by the standards they set.
- Leaders in *blueprint schools* think about the impact of their strategic decisions on other schools and other school leaders.
- The more *blueprint school* leaders choose to put *staff first*, the easier it will become for other school leaders to do the same.

Afterword
The Blueprint for our schools in 2030
John Tomsett & Jonny Uttley

When Huntington was inspected in 2017, a battle-hardened Senior HMI (Her Majesty's Inspector) commented that it had made her year spending 30 minutes talking to our NQTs, because they were so enthused and happy in their work. A year later, two civil servants from the DfE's Delivery Unit visited to discuss managing teacher workload. At the end of the day, they asked me how they could sprinkle what we had created at Huntington across the whole school system. 'How could we,' they pondered, 'persuade other headteachers to do these sensible things, rather than some of the punitive practices that exist in our schools at the moment?'

In 2019, Driffield School, a member of the Education Alliance Trust, was graded 'Good' by the regulator, 30 months after it was put into Special Measures. According to the report, 'Driffield School is a friendly and happy place … Staff feel valued and supported and proud to be working in this school.' Driffield School has emerged from the educational depths because school leaders have put *staff first* and supported them at every level to do the work of school improvement. No off-rolling, no triple marking, no gaming the P8 open bucket, no huge changes; just getting the student behaviour system sorted, focusing upon training the staff to be great teachers, reducing anxiety, and removing unnecessary workload. Four weeks before the last possible date the school could be inspected and the day before the Ofsted call, the school had a training day focused on disciplinary literacy. The word 'Ofsted' was not used once.

We have created the cultures that those visitors experienced despite the policy challenges of the previous decade. We have both, as school leaders, swum against the tide, one as a traditional headteacher, the other as a MAT CEO. In 2007, Mourhead and Barber famously said in their McKinsey report that 'the quality of an education system cannot exceed the quality of its teachers'. Yet, despite the warning, one of the legacies of the last ten years is simple and stark: *we do not have enough people in our own country to educate our own children.*

There is much about the Govian reforms I admired. There, I've said it. I admired Gove's decision to oversee the first fall in GCSE and A level pass rates for two generations. I remember being in a local authority headteachers' meeting in 2009 when Ed Balls, then Secretary of State for Children, Schools and Families, had declared that on the 20-odd KPIs he had defined for schools to measure our performance, we were not allowed to set targets for next year that were lower than the previous year's targets. I exploded, to the discomfort of all present, exclaiming, 'We don't work with wood and steel. We work with human beings! When did we start living in a Stalinist state?!' But Gove's focus upon structures was ideological, largely unnecessary, and costly in so many ways.

The thing is, if you want to achieve something on a large scale, you have to take people with you, something Michael Gove just did not understand or was not inspired to pursue. I have often made the point that headteachers need to trust their colleagues more than ever. At our school, we deliver nearly 2,000 lessons each week; I cannot teach them all, so what I have to do is develop my colleagues in a safe school environment that allows them to thrive professionally and personally. It's the only way I keep my job. If he'd followed suit in 2015, Michael Gove might have kept his job too.

Gove's criticism of the educational so-called 'Blob' helped no one. You learn as a leader that criticising people rarely encourages them to improve. I once saw the Tottenham defender Sol Campbell give the ball away to Dennis Wise, who instantly set up a goal for Chelsea. And I can still see Gary Mabbutt, the Tottenham captain, put his arm around the disconsolate young Campbell, as the Chelsea players celebrated around him, and whisper encouragements into his ear. At Huntington, we have embedded into our cultural DNA the fact that 'we are a school which recognises the fallibility of the human condition – we all make mistakes'. At the Education Alliance, we ask leaders to 'earn trust by being reliable, consistent, credible, honest, humble, courageous and kind'.

As Mary Myatt says, 'the children in our schools are humans first, pupils second; our colleagues are humans first, teachers second'.

So we need to change the narrative around education and what it is like to work in our country's state schools. We need to build schools where adults and children can thrive, where we put *staff first*. We need schools where, if you get it right, the job of teaching can inspire sheer joy in entrants to the profession and 'make old hearts fresh' again for those in the twilight of their careers.

Remember, a *blueprint* is 'an early plan or design that explains how something might be achieved'. This book is the first step towards building a more humane school system. We know that our *blueprint* has holes in it. We know it is overly idealistic. We know it is too general at some points and too detailed at others. But every single element of it is rooted in current practice. It is a way of running schools whose time is arriving. And in an increasing number of enlightened schools, that time is already here. Many schools are already putting *staff first*.

STAFF FIRST BLUEPRINT

1. A school culture which unashamedly puts *staff first*;
2. An explicit part of a leader's role will be to minimise anxiety levels and remove all barriers preventing teachers from teaching;
3. The priority will be the staff so that excellent staff wellbeing will be a by-product of making staff workload manageable;
4. Recruitment processes will be thorough, fair and humane;
5. At every stage of their career, teachers will be afforded personalised development opportunities;
6. Training time for staff will be ring-fenced and substantial;
7. Teaching will be evidence informed, with teachers' own experience enhanced by what the evidence tells us has the best chance of working;
8. Every activity teachers undertake will have a golden thread through to improving students' outcomes;

9. Developing teachers' curriculum expertise will be at the heart of the school's professional development programme;

10. Teachers will readily accept the professional obligation to improve their practice;

11. SLT will prioritise improving students' behaviour so that teachers can teach and students can learn in peace;

12. The only time staff will hear the word Ofsted will be when the headteacher tells the staff that the inspectors are due to arrive the following morning;

13. Feedback loops will enable every colleague to contribute to improving the school;

14. Staff will be openly encouraged and actively supported to think of progressing their careers;

15. Policies around teaching and learning will be developed by middle leaders, in an inverted pyramid approach to school hierarchies;

16. Leaders think about the impact of their decisions on the staff and students in the school down the road.

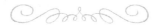

The seed of this book was first planted almost exactly 30 years ago by Roland S. Barth's vision of his 'idealised school culture', from his book, *Improving Schools from Within* (Barth, 1991). I have written about Barth's vision many times. It finishes thus: 'I'd like to work in a school that constantly takes note of the stress and anxiety level on the one hand and standards on the other, all the while searching for the optimal relationship of low anxiety and high standards.' Wouldn't we all? Barth's book has influenced me more than any other educational book I have ever read, and I've read quite a few.

The blurb on the back of Barth's book describes it as 'a humane blueprint for school reform'. Three decades later and three thousand miles across the Atlantic from Cambridge Massachusetts, where Barth wrote his book, this is our own 'humane blueprint' for revitalising England's schools. As well as being a serious proposal to ensure our schools thrive throughout the next decade, it is also, in many ways, a homage to the grounded compassion of Barth's educational philosophy.

Although it will not be easy to change the way we run our schools so that they are humane places where bright, enthused colleagues want to work, it will be a damned sight easier than running our schools without those bright, enthused colleagues.

For the next decade, let's all put *staff first*.

Endnote

Who knew we would be finishing this final edit under national lockdown?

We are both working from home today, overseeing a staff rota for minding the children of workers critical to the country's response to the COVID-19 pandemic.

The response amongst school staff to the crisis has been remarkable. It would be churlish to highlight individual acts of dedication and compassion – we have all contributed.

What is clear is that the true worth of key workers has suddenly hit everyone. And our health workers are beyond compare.

School staff are currently providing them with childcare so that they can save lives. It is our contribution to a national emergency.

Neither of us has been prouder to be school leaders.

We know it is no time to point score. Yet, at one Twitter-moment each, our pride has tipped over into passionate defence of our staff:

John Tomsett
@johntomsett

After the 2 hour meeting I have just had with @HuntingtonYork SLT you'd better not let me ever hear you say, "Them that can, do, and them that can't, teach." Ever.

12:52 PM · Mar 22, 2020 · Twitter for Android

40 Retweets   **255** Likes

Jonny Uttley
@JonnyUttley

We are the front line. Don't anyone EVER make a disparaging comment about a teacher or teaching near me again.

8:46 PM · Mar 23, 2020 · Twitter for iPhone

172 Retweets   **1.5K** Likes

Shakespeare was right when he wrote in *Hamlet*, 'There is nothing either good or bad, but thinking makes it so'. When this is over, when the new normal is established, we just might be a kinder, gentler species, one that realises that we need each other more than we ever knew.

And we just might live in a country that *puts its key workers first*.

John Tomsett, 24 March 2020

Select Bibliography

Curriculum

Allen, Becky & White, Benjamin (4 December 2019) 'Careering towards a curriculum crash', accessed online 20 February 2019 at: https://rebeccaallen.co.uk/2019/12/04/careering-towards-a-curriculum-crash/

Myatt, Mary (2018) *The Curriculum: Gallimaufry to coherence* (Woodbridge: John Catt Educational)

Oates, Tim (2010) *Could Do Better* Cambridge Assessment Research Report (Cambridge, UK: Cambridge Assessment)

Robinson, Martin (2019) *Curriculum: Athena Versus the Machine* (Carmarthen: Crownhouse)

Sealy, Clare, ed. (2020) *The researchED Guide to The Curriculum: An evidence-informed guide for teachers* (Woodbridge: John Catt Educational)

Shulman, Lee S. (1986) 'Those who understand: Knowledge growth in teaching', in *Educational Researcher* 14(2), pp. 4-14 (AERA Presidential Address)

Wiliam, Dylan (2013) 'Redesigning Schooling 3: Principled Curriculum Design' (London: SSAT)

School Leadership

Barth, Roland S. (1991) *Improving Schools from Within: Teachers, parents, and principals can make the difference* (Hoboken, NJ: Jossey-Bass)

Barth, Roland S. (2002) 'The Culture Builder', in *Educational Leadership* 59(8), pp. 6-11

Barton, Geoff (2018) 'In 2018, let's reclaim the career of teaching for what it can be', in *TES*, accessed 20 February 2020 at https://www.tes.com/news/2018-lets-reclaim-career-teaching-what-it-can-be

Bastow Institute, The (2014) 'Open-to-Learning Conversations - Relationships and Trust with Viviane Robinson' on YouTube, accessed 1 March 2020, available at https://www.youtube.com/watch?v=0_I5-HKIR1s&t=58s

Burkeman, Oliver (2013) *The Antidote: Happiness for people who can't stand positive thinking* (Edinburgh: Canongate)

Collins, Jim (2001) *Good to Great* (London: Random House Business)

Crawford, Donna K., Bodine, Richard K. & Hoglund, Robert G. (1993) *The School for Quality Learning: Managing the school and classroom the Deming way* (Champaign, IL: Research Press)

Dickson, John, (2011) *Humilitas* (Michigan: Zondervan)

Fullan, Michael (2008) *The Six Secrets of Change* (San Francisco: Jossey-Bass)

Fullan, Michael (2001) *Leading in a Culture of Change* (San Francisco: Jossey-Bass)

Fullan, Michael (2002) 'The Change Leader', in *Educational Leadership: Beyond Instructional Leadership*, 59(8), pp. 16-21

Fullan, Michael & Hargreaves, Andy (2012) *Professional Capital: Transforming teaching in every school* (New York: Routledge)

Gawunde, Atul (2011) *The Checklist Manifesto: How to get things right* (London: Profile Books)

Munby, Steve (2019) *Imperfect Leadership* (Carmarthen: Crownhouse)

Myatt, Mary (2016) *High Challenge, Low Threat* (Woodbridge: John Catt Educational)

Nicholas, Libby & West-Burnham, John (2016) *Understanding Leadership: Challenges and reflections* (Carmarthen: Crownhouse)

Porritt, Vivienne & Featherstone, Keziah (2019) *10% Braver: Inspiring women to lead education* (London: Sage)

Robertson, Alix (2018) 'Academy autonomy "has no positive impact in the classroom"', in *Schoolsweek*, accessed 20 February 2020 at https://schoolsweek.co.uk/academy-autonomy-has-no-positive-impact-in-the-classroom/

Robinson, Viviane (2018) *Reduce Change to Increase Improvement* (London: Corwin)

Robinson, Viviane (2011) *Student Centred Leadership* (San Francisco: Jossey Bass)

Sharples, Jonathan (2019) *Putting Evidence to Work: A school's guide to implementation*, 2nd edn (London: EEF)

Tomsett, John (2015) *This Much I Know About Love Over Fear: Creating the culture for truly great teaching* (Carmarthen: Crownhouse)

Tschannen-Moran, Megan (2014) *Trust Matters: Leadership for successful schools, 2nd edn* (San Francisco: Jossey Bass)

Wiliam, Dylan (2016) *Leadership for Teacher Learning* (Florida: Learning Sciences International)

Willingham, Daniel T. (2012) *When Can You Trust the Experts? How to tell good science from bad in education* (San Francisco, CA: Jossey-Bass)

Teacher recruitment, training and retention

Allen, Becky & Sims, Sam (2019) *The Teacher Gap* (Abingdon: Routledge)

Barber, Michael & Mourhead, Mona (2007) 'McKinsey Report: How the World's Best-Performing School Systems Come out on Top' (London: McKinsey)

Cordingley, Philippa (2013) 'Enhancing achievement for vulnerable students', AERA, available at http://www.curee.co.uk/publication/enhancing-achievement-vulnerable-students, accessed 24 March 2020

Department for Education (2016) 'Standards for Teachers' Professional Development' (London: DfE)

Department for Education (2019) 'Early Career Framework' (London: DfE)

Eddington, Arthur S. (1935/1959) *New Pathways in Science* (Cambridge: Cambridge University Press)

Fletcher-Wood, Harry, Bignall, Ben, Calvert, Jen, Goodrich, Josh & McCrea, Emma with Efrat Furst (2019) *The Learning Curriculum 2.0* (London: Ambition Institute)

Gibbons, Amy (2018) '"We are driving out creative teachers" says PISA boss', accessed 1 March 2020, available at https://www.tes.com/news/we-are-driving-out-creative-teachers-says-pisa-boss

Hanushek, Eric A. (2010) 'The economic value of higher teacher quality', *Economics of Education Review*, 30(3), pp. 466–479 (Stanford: Elsivier Ltd)

House of Commons (2018) 'Retaining and developing the teaching workforce' (London: House of Commons)

Howard, Kat (2020) *Stop Talking About Wellbeing* (Woodbridge: John Catt Educational)

Kennedy, Mary (2016) 'Parsing the Practice of Teaching', *Journal of Teacher Education*, 67(1), pp. 6-17, accessed 20 February 2020 at https://pdfs.semanticscholar.org/3db0/c7c8485de0511b13652fcfa44d7819ff746e.pdf

Lemov, Doug (2015a) 'Could strategic choice help overcome the mirage?', accessed 20 February 2020 at https://teachlikeachampion.com/blog/strategic-choice-help-overcome-mirage/

Lemov, Doug (2015b) *Teach Like a Champion 2.0* (San Francisco: Jossey Bass)

OECD (2005) *Teachers Matter: Attracting, developing and retaining effective teachers* (Paris: OECD)

Schwartz, Robert B., Wurtzel, Judy & Olson, Lynn (2007) 'Attracting and retaining teachers', *OECD Observer*, 261

Perry, Emily, Booth, Josephine, Owen, David & Bower, Kim (2019) *The Curriculum for Initial Teacher Education: Literature Review* (Sheffield: Sheffield Hallam University) https://assets.publishing.service.gov.uk/government/uploads/system/uploads/attachment_data/file/839656/Literature_Review_of_Initial_Teacher_Education_Curriculum_-_final.pdf

Pink, Daniel (2011) *Drive: The surprising truth about what motivates us* (New York: Riverhead Books)

Rosenthal, J., Routch, K., Monahan, K. & Doherty, M. (2018) "The holy grail of effective leadership succession planning", *Deloitte Insights*, available at https://www2.deloitte.com/insights/us/en/topics/leadership/effective-leadership-succession-planning.html, accessed, 17 February 2020

Ward, Helen (2017) 'Teaching in England is not "interesting" enough says PISA boss', *TES*, 20 September 2017

Weston, David (2020) 'Is there evidence for CPD', available at https://tdtrust.org/is-there-evidence-for-cpd, accessed 24 March 2020

Whitehall Study I (1967) and Whitehall II (1984); see Whitehall II (also known as the 'Stress and Health Study') at http://www.ucl.ac.uk/whitehallII/

Wiliam, Dylan (2014) 'Why teaching will never be an evidence based profession', presentation researchED 2014, available at https://www.dylanwiliam.org/Dylan_Wiliams_website/Presentations.html, accessed 24 March 2020

Worth, J. & Van den Brande, J. (2020) 'Teacher autonomy: how does it relate to job satisfaction and retention?' (Slough: NFER)

Teaching and learning

Benton, T. (2016) 'Comparable Outcomes: Scourge or Scapegoat?', Cambridge Assessment Research Report (Cambridge, UK: Cambridge Assessment)

Berger, Ron (2003) *An Ethic of Excellence: Building a culture of craftsmanship with students* (Portsmouth, NH: Heinemann)

Boxer, Adam, ed. (2019) *The researchED Guide to Explicit & Direct Instruction: An evidence-informed guide for teachers* (Abingdon: Routledge)

Busch, Bradley (2019) *The Science of Learning: 77 Studies That Every Teacher Needs to Know* (Abingdon: Routledge)

Caviglioli, Oliver (2019) *Dual Coding with Teachers* (Woodbridge: John Catt Educational)

Christodoulou, Daisy (2017) *Making Good Progress? The future of assessment for learning* (Oxford: OUP)

Education Endowment Foundation (2019) 'Improving Behaviour in our Schools' (London: EEF)

Hattie, John (2011) *Visible Learning for Teachers: Maximizing impact on learning* (London: Routledge)

Hendrick, Carl (2018) *What does this look like in the classroom?* (Woodbridge: John Catt Educational)

Jones, Kate (2019) *Retrieval Practice* (Woodbridge: John Catt Educational)

Kvarven, A., Strømland, E., Wollbrant, C. et al (2020) "The intuitive cooperation hypothesis revisited: a meta-analytic examination of effect size and between-study heterogeneity" in the *Journal of the Economic Science Association* (2020), available at https://doi.org/10.1007/s40881-020-00084-3, accessed 24 March 2020

Lemov, Doug (2010) *Teach Like a Champion: 49 techniques that put students on the path to college* (San Francisco, CA: Jossey-Bass)

McCourt, Mark (2019) *Teaching for Mastery* (Woodbridge: John Catt Educational)

Muijs, Daniel & Reynolds, David (2017) *Effective Teaching: Evidence and practice*, 4th edn (London: Sage)

Nuthall, Graham (2007) *The Hidden Lives of Learners* (New Zealand: NZCER)

Pullan, Sam (2019) 'Students have teachers figured out in 2 seconds', *Teachwire*, accessed on 20 February 2020 at https://www.teachwire.net/news/students-have-teachers-figured-out-in-just-2-seconds

Quigley, Alex (2018) *Closing the Vocabulary Gap* (Woodbridge: John Catt Educational)

Quigley, Alex (2020a) *Closing the Reading Gap* (Woodbridge: John Catt Educational)

Quigley, Alex (2020b) 'Curriculum Development and Teacher Development', accessed 29 February 2020, available at https://www.theconfidentteacher.com/2020/02/curriculum-development-and-teacher-development/

Robinson, Martin (2013) *The Trivium* (Carmarthen: Crownhouse)

Rowland, Marc (2019) 'Unlocking talent, fulfilling potential – Social Mobility in York', keynote speech, 25 September 2019, STEM centre, York

Sherrington, Tom (2015) 'Nicky Morgan vs the Bell Curve', accessed 1 March 2020, available at https://teacherhead.com/2015/06/30/nicky-morgan-vs-the-bell-curve/

Sherrington, Tom (2016) 'Rethinking Success in the Post-Gaming Zero Sum Era', accessed 1 March 2020, available at https://teacherhead.com/2016/06/28/rethinking-success-in-the-post-gaming-zero-sum-era/

Sherrington, Tom (2017) *The Learning Rainforest* (Woodbridge: John Catt Educational)

Sherrington, Tom (2019) *Rosenshine's Principles in Action* (Woodbridge: John Catt Educational)

Sherrington, Tom & Caviglioli, Oliver (2020) *Teaching WalkThrus: Five step guides for instructional coaching* (Woodbridge: John Catt Educational)

Shulman, Lee S. (2004) *The wisdom of practice: Essays on teaching, learning, and learning to teach* (San Francisco: Jossey-Bass)

Slabakova, Roumyana (2018) 'The Bottleneck Hypothesis Updated' 10.1075/lald.63.16sla

Thomson, Dave (2019a) 'Progress 8 scores for most schools are not that different', accessed 1 March 2020, available at https://ffteducationdatalab.org.uk/2019/02/progress-8-scores-for-most-schools-arent-that-different/

Thomson, Dave (2019b) 'Are some qualifications scored too generously?', accessed 1 March 2020, available at https://ffteducationdatalab.org.uk/2019/09/are-some-qualifications-scored-too-generously/

Weinstein, Yana (2019) *Understanding how we learn: a visual guide* (Abingdon: Routledge)

Willingham, Daniel (2010) *Why Don't Students Like School?* (San Francisco: Jossey Bass)

Blogs and Websites

Alex Quigley: www.theconfidentteacher.com
Ambition Institute: www.ambition.org.uk
Becky Allen: www.rebeccaallen.co.uk
Ben White: www.benjamindwhite.wordpress.com
Carl Hendrick: www.chronotopeblog.com
Christine Counsell: www.thedignityofthethingblog.wordpress.com
Claire Stoneman: www.birminghamteacher.wordpress.com
Daisy Christodoulou: www.daisychristodoulou.com
Daniel Willingham: www.danielwillingham.com
Deans for Impact: www.deansforimpact.org
Education Endowment Foundation: www.educationendowmentfoundation.org.uk
Huntington Research School: www.researchschool.org.uk/huntington
John Tomsett: www.johntomsett.com
Laura McInerney: www.lauramcinerney.com
Mary Myatt: www.marymyatt.com
National Association of School-Based Teacher Trainers:
www.nasbtt.org.uk/teacher-educator-programmes
Steve Rollett: www.stephenrollett.com
Tom Sherrington: www.teacherhead.com
Wolds Associate Research School: www.southhunsley.org.uk

Twitter

Adam Boxer: @adamboxer1
Alex Quigley: @HuntingEnglish
Carl Hendrick: @C_Hendrick
Christine Counsell: @Counsell_C
Claire Stoneman: stoneman_claire
Clare Sealy: @ClareSealy
Deans for Impact: @deansforimpact
Jon Hutchinson: @jon_hutchinson_
Jonathan Sharples: @sharples_j
Jonny Uttley: @JonnyUttley
Laura McInerney: @miss_mcinerney
Marc Enser: @EnserMark
Martin Robinson: @Trivium21c
Mary Myatt: @MaryMyatt
Michael Fordham: @mfordhamhistory
Ruth Walker: @rosalindphys
Sam Twiselton: @samtwiselton
Steve Rollett: @steverollett
Tom Sherrington: @Teacherhead

CPSIA information can be obtained
at www.ICGtesting.com
Printed in the USA
JSHW041540220920
8135JS00004B/8